Vibrant Life Cookbook
Recipes that heal & strengthen your body, mind & spirit

From the author of *Anatomy of Healing & Wellness*
and creator of the *Vibrant Life Protocol™*

Testimonials

Absolutely Delicious and I Feel So Healthy!

"Thank you Sheila for sharing your wisdom with all of us. Your recipes are easy for me to follow and 100% of the time they've turned out amazingly delicious! I also love knowing that I'm nourishing my body so profoundly and learning about all the different ingredients and how they heal. My parents are especially picky eaters and typically enjoy foods that are so bad for them which just kills me. They actually love your food and it's making them healthier! That means the world to me. Today for lunch I had one of your really nice Bean Burritos. The twist of lime added something so wonderful to the flavor! I've also recently made the broccoli soup and butternut squash soup with one of your Arugula salads and homemade dressings. Absolutely delicious and I always feel amazingly healthy for it. Thank you for all that you do Sheila!

—Tom Birkenmeyer
International Internet Blogger & Professional Network Marketer
www.TomBirkenmeyer.com

"Delicious and Life Changing Recipes"

I came to Dr. Sheila Z and *True Life Solutions* because I was looking for a purely natural solution to my health issues, most specifically candida and asthma. She came very highly recommended. My candida issue was becoming worse, to the point that my adrenals were flat lining. I was falling asleep while driving and taking naps in my car when I got home because I was just too tired to even get out of the car and go into the house. It was affecting every aspect of my life. I started Dr. Sheila's '*Vibrant Life Protocol*' which she designed specifically for ME, based on many factors of MY body type MY blood type, current eating habits, physical ailments, etc. Unlike my primary doctor that would prescribe a pill for what ailes me, she started me on a 'clean' meal plan with simple, delicious dishes, and even showed me (in person) how to prepare healthy recipes. After only 90 days on the protocol, I had my blood professionally tested again with incredible results. My stamina improved, my memory improved and I wake up every day now with energy that I haven't had in years. I can only attribute it to her protocol and clean eating program. I am so excited that some of these recipes will now be in Dr. Sheila Z's *Vibrant Life Cook Book*! I can't wait to get my copy and it will make a perfect gift for those I care about. Thank you, Dr. Sheila for these delicious life changing recipes!

—Karen Eastman

Amazing & Healing Chicken Soup

Your Grandma's Chicken Soup recipe has become a family tradition. I just love your secret ingredient, parsnips! It adds such an amazing flavor and consistency. I followed your cooking video at: www.truelife-solutions.com/healthy-kitchen-connection. It is so interesting to learn about why Organic Chicken Legs are the key to optimal nutritional bio availability of K2. I also love the fact you put a "vegan" option in your informative *Vibrant Life Cookbook*. From Grandma's Chicken Soup to your famous Raspberry Sorbet, this is a must for everyone's kitchen who wants to eat consciously.

—Victoria Goldie Amira RDH

A Wonderful Way to Eat

I'm so excited about Sheila Z's recipe book, so that more people can experience "clean" eating. You'll get many different recipes to support you in your health. ***Please read my story:*** I have two stints due to experiencing a heart attack in February of 2013. I decided to NOT take any drugs, which meant I had to control my blood flow with food, supplements, and exercise. With Sheila's help, I was able to accomplish that. I had been on a specific food and supplement regime for a couple of years before meeting Sheila. However, when I found out how knowledgeable she is, I decided to go on her 90 day protocol. I felt as though I just needed to do MORE to get my body in optimum balance. After taking several blood and other tests, Sheila created a custom program for me. She gave me specific foods and supplements to take to get ALL of my numbers down to (or up) to where they needed to be. When we first started I had some plaque, sugar crystals, radical white cells, and a couple of other issues that needed to be handled. Sheila has cooked some of her recipes for me. She also gave me many recipes that supported me in getting my issues handled. No more plaque, sugar crystals, or radical white blood cells was the result shown in tests. I recommend you get Sheila's recipe book so you can eat "clean" and get in optimum balance. Of course, I would also recommend working with Sheila on her 90 day protocol too.

—Cheri Hickman

Reconnective Healing® Foundational Practitioner Joyologist

Vibrant Life Cookbook

by Sheila Z. Stirling PhD

Copyright ©2016

Cover Design/Interior layout by
Dianne Rux - DzinerGraphics.com
Cover Photo by Michael W. Rogers
www.MichaelWardieRogers.com

Wisdom Press Publishing

4132 S. Rainbow Blvd. #465

Las Vegas, NV 89108

www.wisdompresspublishing.com

Sheila Z. Stirling, PhD

ISBN 978-0-9911026-1-7

Library of Congress: 2016

Printed in the United States of America

"Prevention is the Name of the Game"

Staying young and vibrant is a reality, not a dream.
The saying *"you are what you eat"* turns out to be the truth.

Everyday we make choices; what to wear, what we feel,
what to eat. Every moment is a choice.
More and more we seem to know people who are ill or
trying desperately to recover from being ill or
dealing with the grief of loosing someone who was ill.

You do hold the keys to a healthy vibrant life and my cookbook
is dedicated to getting the word and these healthy healing
recipes out to the world. Yes, it may take a bit more time to find
the clean foods, herbs and high quality ingredients that are
among these pages,
YOU ARE WORTH IT!

Because it is true that, *"Your Health is Your Wealth."*
Start today to feel (and see) your amazing life
become even more amazing.

This book is dedicated to YOU!
Sheila Z. Stirling, PhD

Table of Contents

Why is the Vibrant Life Cookbook so different?

The main difference is, it has a wide variety of origins. All healthy organic of course and mostly medicinal. It was thousands of years ago that Hypocrites said *"Let thy food be thy medicine"* All the recipes in the *Vibrant Life Cookbook* will enhance your well being and strengthen your immune system. And for those who have experienced the Vibrant Life Protocol™, now know from experience that food can be your medicine. Also you will notice that many recipes have herbal options that will add a bit more muscle to your delicious dish.

In addition I have listed specific foods that are healing and good for specific organs in your body. Information is key when you are ready to change your wellness status for the better. Regardless if you are 20 or 90, this cookbook is unique and on the cutting edge of wellness.

My motto is "Stay 30 til' you are 90" and this is a large part of the secret.

Please note that *The Vibrant Life Cook Book* is not affiliated with the protocol. Yes, some of the foods are used in the protocol however, the protocol is very targeted and individually created per each individual's requirements. The protocol is all about cleaning up the blood in 90 -100 days, and some amazing results have been seen and felt by those embarking on the program.

The Vibrant Life Cook Book includes Raw recipe's, Vegan Recipes, Vegetarian Recipes, Gluten Free and even one that has an organic meat option. It may not be one way, but all ways that bring us to ecstatic wellness.

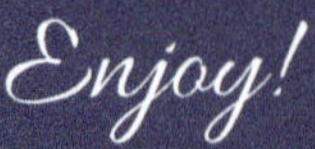

Egg Feta Wrap 14

Raw Oatmeal 16

Egg Feta Veggie Cups 18

Gluten & Toxic Free Pancakes 20

Avocado Toast 22

Onion & Yellow Pepper Scramble 24

Many say breakfast is the most important meal of the day. Why do they say that? Just like your car, your body needs fuel to run properly. The body needs some sort of protein, green veggies for enzymes, and perhaps the very first thing in the morning is 1/2 organic lemon squeezed into a glass of warm water. Why? Because lemon juice, although an acid, turns alkaline when ingested. The lemon water wakes up your liver and organs in a good way. It helps break down mucus in the body and it aids in controlling bad bacteria in your gut. It also helps maintain healthy eyes. So, yes to "Healthy Beginnings" every day.

New beginnings

Egg Feta Wrap

This healthy sprouted wrap is great for a morning meal or anytime of day.

Ingredients:

- 1 large Ezekiel tortilla
- 1 egg fried in organic butter
- 1 Tbs Feta cheese *(to your taste)*
- 1 or 2 Tbs Brushetta

(Trader Joe's is my favorite)

- 2 Tbs Grapeseed Oil
- 1/4 cup Arugula

Recipe for homemade Brushetta on page 76

Method:

Step 1: Place between 1 - 2 Tbs *(or less)* Grapeseed oil to coat your frying pan.

Step 2: Heat the tortilla in the coated pan on medium heat.

Step 3: Turn again and again, so it doesn't get too crispy.

Fry your egg in a separate pan, break the yolk and cook the egg thoroughly.

Step 4: When the tortilla is done to your satisfaction, put the tortilla on a plate and place the fried egg on it.

Step 5: Add the brushetta, and crumble a bit of Feta cheese on top.

Step 6: Top off with fresh organic Arugula.

Roll the tortilla and enjoy this amazing
and oh-so-yummy wrap!

Option:

If you don't have brushetta handy and would like a South-of-the-Border flair, a Tbs of Trader Joe's Salsa Verde makes a delicious option.

Tip:

Arugula is considered a bitter.
And is *oh-so-good* for your liver.
This yummy wrap is
a family favorite.

Raw Oatmeal Breakfast

This high antioxidant meal is a smart way to start the day.
Raw oatmeal is great for you.

Ingredients:

- 1/3 cup (or one heaping handful) organic rolled oats

Method:

Step 1: Place the oats in a bowl and add in a bit of water to soak the oats. Let them sit for about 3-5 min. Drain excess water and stir the oats just a bit.

Step 2: Now add your organic blueberries, raspberries, raisins and occasionally use half of a banana.

Option: Add a bit of local organic honey to taste. I also like to pour about a 1/3 cup of almond/coconut milk on top. Use organic Stevia if you are concerned about your blood sugar.

This raw breakfast will help your cholesterol levels, is healthy for your heart, your blood and your clarity of mind.

Be sure to buy organic fruits. It is well worth the extra price
to insure that you help to minimize consumed toxins.

Tip: Raisins have iron, bananas have potassium
and berries are high in antioxidants.
A hand full of organic raw oats is the perfect amount for you.
Use a measuring cup if you must, or measure just how
much your hand will hold. That's your perfect amount.

Gluten Free Egg Feta Veggie Cups

A great way to start your day. These on-the-go egg cups will last for days in your refrigerator. Although, we all know eating them fresh from the oven is the best way to enjoy them. In a hurry? Kids late for school? Here is an easy and nutritious answer.

Preheat oven to 350 degrees.
Coat your muffin cups with butter or use paper/parchment cup liners.
Put a bit of water in the empty cups before you place in the oven.
If you are using just a few eggs, you will have empty cups!

Ingredients:

- 10 - 12 free range organic eggs *(preferred)*
- 1/2 to 1 cup of chopped spinach *(to your desired taste)*
- 1/2 tsp *(or less)* mineral or Celtic salt
- 1 Tbs of Feta cheese, crumbled
  Adding a bit of chopped yellow pepper really boosts the taste! Try it!

Method:

Step 1:	In a large bowl beat 10 - 12 free range organic eggs *(preferred)*.
Step 2:	Add the remaining ingredients.
Step 3:	Put a bit of butter in the baking cups, pour mixture into baking cups.
Step 4:	Bake for about 20 - 25 minutes at 350 degrees.
Step 5:	Test with a knife, if it comes out dry, they are done.

Allow to cool just a couple of minutes and serve.

Note:

You can also add chopped green or red pepper, onion or chives for some great flavor variations. Orange or Yellow Bell Pepper is our family favorite!

Tip:
Please choose "free range" organic for the best quality eggs and always use organic or Kerri Gold butter. The vegan option is to use Grapeseed oil.

Glutin & Toxin Free Pancakes

Ingredients:

- 1 cup brown rice flour
  I use Bob's Red Mill Organic Whole Grain Brown Rice Flour.
- 2 tsp aluminum-free baking powder
- 1 egg
- 1 cup almond or almond/coconut Milk
- 2 Tbs organic butter

- 1 Tbs coconut oil
- 1/2 tsp Xylitol
- 1 - 2 tsp evaporated cane, organic palm sugar or 1/4 tsp Stevia *optional*
- 5 drops of pure vanilla
- 1/4 tsp salt *(I use pink Himalayan)*

Method:

Step 1:   In a glass or stainless steel large bowl place the Almond milk and egg and whisk till smooth.

Step 2:   Then add the sugar and Xylitol, melted butter, coconut oil and salt.

Step 3:   Whisk till smooth.

Step 4:   Add the vanilla and baking powder, whisk till smooth.

Step 5:   Slowly add the flour and whisk till all is blended and smooth.

Step 6:   Heat skillet on medium heat. Use a bit of butter to coat the pan.

Use about 1/4 cup *(or a bit less or more)* of the batter per pancake.
Use a stainless steel spatula for best results.

Step 7:   Allow bubbles to appear and burst. When bubbles are in the middle of the pancake it is ready to turn over for a minute or two. Check for the perfect color.

This makes about 5 large pancakes and not a speck of gluten!

Please use organic maple syrup to top off this delicious and traditional breakfast .

Tip:
Brown rice flour retains all of the whole grain when ground and that keeps the fiber content up in this gluten free flour. This in turn is much better for your glucose levels than white rice flour or any other flour. It is also high in B vitamins and in protein. Brown rice flour gets a two thumbs up in my book!

Avocado Toast

Starting the day with protein and high omega 3 is a great way to cover your nutritional goals for the day. Avocado is high in Omega 3 and an egg is high in protein. It seems so simple, so let's give it a try.

Ingredients:

- Egg(s) fried, poached or however you like them
- 1/2 to 1 avocado
- Squeeze of lemon
- Salt and pepper to taste

I like to use Ezekiel bread to toast, because it is organic sprouted grains and has NO flour in it. A low glycemic index in comparison to regular breads, and also gluten free. You may use any toast you like, but, please use organic butter.

Method:

Step 1:   Simply toast your bread.

Step 2:   Mash 1/2 avocado and spread on bread.

Step 3:   Place your fried or poached egg on top. Sprinkle a bit of mineral salt and pepper and wa-la!!!

You may squeeze a bit of lemon on the avocado if you like. Some people like to sprinkle it with a bit of cayenne. This is optional of course.

This also makes a great afternoon snack.

Tip:

Avocado is high in omega 3 and the "good fat" topped with the protein of the egg and you have a winning dish that will strengthen your system.

Gluten Free Onion & Yellow Pepper Scramble

Serving size 1 person

Ingredients:

- 1 or 2 farm fresh eggs
- 1 Tbs yellow onion or chives
- 1 or 2 Tbs yellow bell pepper chopped into small pieces
- 1/3 tsp or a pinch of Celtic salt finely ground
- 1/2 to 1 Tbs organic butter

Method:

Step 1: Beat eggs.

Step 2: Saute the onion and yellow bell pepper in skillet with a bit of organic butter, until tender, just a minute or two.

Step 3: Pour the eggs into the buttered skillet.

Step 4: Use a wooden spoon or a spatula to move the mix around until your eggs are at your perfect level of being done.

Step 5: Plate your healthy breakfast and enjoy.
(Salsa Verde' is de-lish as a garnish)

Why Onions & Peppers?

Onions contain flavonoids that have a direct affect as an anti-tumor agent. Onions are great for your immune system and contain Quercitin, that is great for raising the good HDL cholesterol, and helps to fight off bronchitis, hay fever, and diabetes. Onions are anti-inflammatory, antiviral and are known to be anti cancer. Need I say more?

So, bell peppers of any color are a great and healthy addition.

Bell Peppers are high in Vitamin A which helps to support your eyes. They contain lutein that may lower your risk of macular degeneration. Vitamin C, as we all know, is great for our skin and our immune system. Vitamin K is good for our blood and over all health. Also, B6 and folate which helps to lower homocysteine and may reduce the risk of heart disease. They also help to activate your metabolic system and can assist in weight shedding.

Tip:
You can use any color
bell pepper you desire.
This nutritious meal can
be enjoyed any time of
day or evening.

We burn the most calories during the day. If you feel like a hearty meal, now is the time. Any carbs are best enjoyed mid day as your body will burn off the excess glucose it receives from bread, or pasta, etc. It is also important to do a bit of "earthing" at this time. Can you eat outside? Place your feet on the earth? Or have picnic, on the lawn or a park bench? Go the extra mile, your body will say, *thank you* in so many wonderful ways.

Let's do Lunch

"If your going to have carbs, now's the time.
Have your largest, main meal in the middle of the day.
Your body will say, *thank you* at night."

Spicy Raw Wrap

The Raw Wrap exclusive recipe from the owner of the "Go Vegan" Restaurants.

Ingredients:

- 2 cup sunflower seeds
- 1 cup pumpkin seeds
- 1/4 cup lemon Juice
- 2 Tbs Bragg's Liquid Aminos
- 1 1/2 Tbs Cumin Powder
- 1 tsp salt
  (less, if you're watching salt intake)

- 1/8 cup garlic cloves
- 1/2 Habanera *(or less, to your taste)*
- 1 cup purified water
- 4 collard green leaves

You are welcomed to sprout your seeds by soaking them overnight.
The seeds do not have enzyme inhibitors so, it is not mandatory to soak them.
The photo of this wrap is one collard green leaf cut into 4 pieces.
Feel free to cut the amounts above in half!

Method:

Step 1: Place all ingredients (except water) into a food processor
Then, add water gradually until desired consistency.

Step 2: Spread the mixture on a collard green leaf.
Top with guacamole and salsa.

Step 3: Roll into a wrap and enjoy!

You may use Romaine, cabbage, or any wrap of your choice.
Use it as a dip with your favorite veggies.

Thank you Lu V. for this amazing and yummy "Go Raw Cafe" lunch classic recipe.
We love your *Go Raw Cafe* and your new *Go Vegan Cafe*.
www.govegan.cafe "Go Raw Cafe" classic recipe.

White Bean Avocado Wrap

One of my favorite healthy kitchen recipes and it's VEGAN as well!!

Ingredients:

- 1 can white beans *(I like to use organic white kidney beans or Cannellini beans canned from Trader Joe's)*
- Thinly sliced red onion
- 1 Tbs organic cumin *(or to taste)*
- Thinly sliced yellow pepper *(one or 2 thin slices is great for a wrap)*

- 1/2 avocado sliced
- 1 Tbs green salsa *(I use Trader Joe's green salsa. About 1 Tbs or to taste)*
- 1 Ezekiel tortilla
- 1 - 2 Tbs Grapeseed oil

Method:

Step 1: Heat the beans, and add in the cumin.

Step 2: While the beans are heating, cut up the avocado, yellow pepper and onion slices.

Step 3: Put the Grapeseed oil in a frying pan. *(stainless steel is best)* In a separate pan heat the tortilla turning it often so as to keep it soft.

Step 4: Sometimes, I will take the time to saute' the onions and peppers as seen in the photo.

Step 5: When the tortilla(s) are hot, place it on a plate. First place the beans on, then the vegetables.

Step 6: Top it with some green salsa and you have a delicious, nutritious lunch.

Tip: Did you know white beans have about 8 grams of protein per 1/2 cup? Avocado is full of the omega's our body needs and onions have incredible healing properties for the body. The Ezekiel tortilla is sprouted grains and so it is gluten free. How can this healthy goodness be so tasty? Try it and find out. Enjoy!

Green Beans in Coconut Puree

An amazing side or lunch dish from Chef Johnny Brannigan

Green beans in creamed coconut puree of vegetables are popular in Indian cuisine. Using green beans is more rare, but intensely flavorful and an enticing green emerald color. It's perfect eaten with a paratha or a puree. Green beans balance all 3 doshas.

Ingredients

- 1/2 lb. fresh green beans top and tailed and chopped small water
- 2 Tbs almond or sunflower oil
- 2 Tbs Chef Johnny's Pitta seasoning *(pg 156)*
- 2 Tbs cumin seed
- 1 Tbs lemon juice

- 2 Tbs dried coconut
- 3 Tbs coconut cream
- 3 Tbs almond cream
- 2 Tbs chopped cilantro leaves
- 2 tsp grated ginger
- Salt and black pepper to taste

Method:

Step 1: Steam the beans in a small amount of water until tender. *(9 -12 mins. approximately)*

Step 2: Meanwhile in a small frying pan, heat the oil and saute the cumin seed until golden brown. Add cumin and grated ginger and stir until they start to brown slightly.

Step 3: Add the coconut, let it change color and add the Pitta seasoning.

Step 4: Stir and add the coconut cream and lemon juice.

Step 5: Stir in the almond cream and then remove from the heat.

Step 6: Add the cooked beans and 1 Tbs cooking liquid from the pan.

Step 7: Blend half the contents into a puree, it should be thick like a paste.

Step 8: Add the cilantro.

Step 9: Mix the puree with the remaining beans.

Serve with rice, kitchari or bread.

Johnny Brannigan
www.vedicchef.com

How to make Almond Cream

Instructions from The Vedic Chef Johnny Brannigan on

Almond Cream

- 10 blanched almonds

  (drop into boiling water for 2 min, drain and the skins come off)
- Place the blanched almonds in a magic bullet or blender add
- 1/4 cup water

Method:

Blend in a blender or magic bullet until smooth and you have almond cream. Thick and smooth.

Gluten Free Baked Zucchini

Ingredients:

- 1 or 2 large well-formed zucchini
- 2 - 3 Tbs bruschetta

  (I use Trader Joe's as I just love it! However, you can make your own. See page 76)
- A bit of Parmesan cheese, or vegan cheese if you are vegan

Method:

Step 1: Slice the raw zucchini in half-lengthwise and place on a foil covered cookie sheet or baking pan.

Step 2: Cover the slices with a generous amount of bruschetta and sprinkle Parmesan cheese on top.

If you are vegan, omit the cheese or use vegan cheese.

Step 3: Place about 1/2 cup of water in the bottom of baking dish.

Bake in a preheated oven of 350 degrees for about 30 minutes.

Cheese will be melted or crust like and zucchini will be soft when poked with a fork. Cool for a few minutes and you have a delicious and elegant side dish, snack or small meal.

Tip: Zucchini's are very low in calories, not that we count calories. They are also high on the anti-oxidant scale and have lots of potassium and folate to offer. This dish is also good cold. Although, I prefer it hot out of the oven and cooled just a bit. Makes a great and healthy side dish as well.

Gluten Free Macaroni & Raw Veggies

Brown rice noodles seem to be the closest I have found to old fashioned noodles in the way of texture and taste.

Ingredients:

- 1 cup brown rice macaroni
- 1/2 yellow pepper *chopped fine*
- 1 green or 1/3 red onion *chopped fine*
- 1/2 small zucchini *chopped small*
- 1 - 2 stalks chopped celery
- 1/2 organic lemon squeezed
- 1/2 Granny Smith apple *chopped fine*

- 1 hard boiled egg
  (organic free range please)
- 1 Tbs organic mayonnaise or vegenaise
- 1 tsp oil - I use almond oil. *You may use your favorite oil*
- Handful of red grapes *(optional)*
- Half pear chopped fine *(optional)*

I also added a bit of chopped fine spinach.

Method

Step 1:	Boil the macaroni to desired softness. About 12 - 15 minutes or so.
Step 2:	Drain and set aside in a bowl.
Step 3:	Add the lemon and the oil.
Step 4:	Then add all the vegetables and lightly stir.
Step 5:	Add the mayonnaise and the grapes. *(or half of a pear)*

The grapes add a bit of sweetness.
I like to slice a hard boiled egg and put on top.

You can also chop the egg up, it adds protein and other good nutrients.

This make enough for 2 people and a refreshing lunch full of raw vegetable goodness.

Tip: This is the Z version of Macaroni Salad someone once said. Lots of variety of vegetables and the grapes really top it off. Feel free to put your favorite fruit or veggie in as well.

Stuffed Pepper Lunch

Ingredients:

- 1 bell pepper *(red, yellow or green)*
- 1 cup cooked Quinoa *(You may also use brown rice)*
- 1 carrot *(chopped or finely shredded)*
- 1/2 avocado chopped
- 1/4 cup peas
- Green onion
- Red grapes
- A few shakes of Red Top Spike seasoning.

Optional: 1 - 2 tsp of Brannigan's seasonings, I use Kappa for this dish *(pg 156)*
Use 1/2-1 Tbs of olive or almond oil, if the mixture seems dry.

Method:

Step 1: Place Quinoa in a pot with about 1-2 cups water. Let simmer for about 20 min. until all the moisture is absorbed.

Step 2: Cut pepper in half.

Step 3: Clean out all seeds and membrane, rinse and set aside.

Step 4: Chop all the ingredients fine, and add to the Quinoa or brown rice.

Step 5: Scoop the filling into each half.

Optional Method: In the last few minutes of cooking the Quinoa, add the vegetables to the Quinoa to soften them up and this also brings out the flavor of the vegetables. This makes this a Raw lunch (or not so raw lunch)... you decide.
You can also add the seasonings and the oil to the Quinoa (or brown rich) and it creates a sauce like flavor.

You can also put this in a hot oven for a few minutes with vegan cheese on top.
Optional: *A bit of olive oil and about 1/2 an orange squeezed makes*
for a very tasty and nutritious lunch.

Super Sandwich

There's nothing like a yummy sandwich to tame a hungry tummy.

Ingredients:

- 2 slices of gluten free bread *(like Ezekiel or your favorite whole grain bread)*
- 1/2 cucumber
- 1/2 avocado
- 1/2 pear
- 1/4 yellow pepper

- 1/3 zucchini *(peeled)*
- 1 Tbs plain yogurt
- 1/2 tsp dried or fresh dill
- 1 tsp + almond milk

Optional:
1 Tbs organic mayonnaise
About 1/2 cup finely grated organic beets

Method:

Step 1: Thinly *(very thinly)* slice the cucumber, avocado, pear, zucchini and yellow pepper.

Step 2: Mix the plain yogurt, dill and almond milk until the consistency of a sauce, set aside.

Step 3: Coat your bread with mayonnaise and spread the dill sauce on both sides of the bread.

Step 4: Carefully place the sliced vegetables onto the bread and enjoy your super sandwich.

This is a delightful way to eat your vegetables. If you would like to add a protein, Boars Head Turkey slices or heated Tempe goes great with this Super Veggie Sandwich.

The Beet: Finely grate the beet and have it on the side. It adds a great sweet flavor to this fulfilling lunch.

Salads are a great way to combine lots of dark green foods and other nutritionally dense foods, like onions, avocados, celery, green apple, pear, tomatoes, beets and the list goes on and on.
Don't forget, you need protein! Whatever you use for protein, now is the time to eat it. Follow some of my healthy dressing recipes as this is the area that usually ups the calories and toxins for a salad. There are many great and tasty ways to dress up your greens.
One could also say, *"A salad a day keeps illness away!"*

Simply Salads

"When in doubt? Have a salad.
Great for digestion and dense in nutrition.
Arugula is a bitter and good for your liver.
A great way to get your "raw" on. Yeah!!"

Arugula & Pear Salad

Salad Ingredients:

- 2 cups organic baby Arugula - cut up
- 1 pear cut up
- 1 Tbs Feta cheese

Dressing:

- Organic olive oil
- Organic lemon *(to taste)*
- A pinch of 100% organic Stevia

Pour over salad and toss!

Optional:

You can change the taste of the salad by using half a Granny Smith apple cut up. Also, watermelon or avocado add some wonderful flavor variations to this salad.

I find the basic dressing above is the best for this afternoon or evening delight.

Tip: Recent studies have shown that the skin of pears contains at least three to four times as many phenolic phytonutrients as the flesh. These phytonutrients include antioxidant, anti-inflammatory flavonoids, and potentially anti-cancer phytonutrients like cinnamic acids. The skin of the pear has also been shown to contain about half of the pear's total dietary fiber. The flavonoids in pears are also known to improve insulin sensitivity. All of this is great news as stated on whfoods.org.

Cold Quinoa Salad

Super charge your salad with this "super grain" Quinoa

Salad Ingredients:

- 1 cup Quinoa
  (I mix multi colored and plane)
- 1 - 2 cups water
- 1 Tbs Ayurvedic Spices (page 156)
  or Turmeric
- Pinch of salt
- Raisins *(optional, if you like a bit of sweet)*
- 2 stalks of green onion or shallots
- 1/2 of a yellow bell pepper
- 1/3 of a cucumber
- 1/2 Granny Smith apple chopped fine
- 2 stalks of celery finely chopped

You can also add mandarin oranges or red bell pepper if you like.
I like to top it off with some fresh basil chopped fine

Optional: Use 1/2 - 1 Tbs of olive or almond oil, if the mixture seems dry.

Method:

Step 1: Bring water to a boil with the Quinoa salt, spices and turmeric.

Step 2: Boil on low until all the liquid is absorbed and Quinoa is soft. (about 20 min.)

Step 3: Add in the raisins during the last 5 minutes so they get plump and soft.

Step 4: Add in the vegetables.

Allow to cool. Or, put in refrigerator until cold.

Step 5: Squeeze about half lemon and 1 Tbs extra virgin olive oil over the salad. Mix together and serve.

Optional:

Try some cut up watermelon or red grapes in this dish, very yummy!
A great cold nutritious salad!

Brown Rice & Broccoli Salad

Chick peas are high in protein and also help regulate insulin levels.

Ingredients:

- 2 cups organic Romaine lettuce - chopped *(you may use Arugula if you prefer)*
- 1 cup broccoli florets - cut up into bite size
- 1 cup organic brown rice - steamed *(use warm or cool as you like)*
- 1/4 cup silvered raw almonds
- 1/2 - 1 cup garbanzo beans *(I use Trader Joe's canned)*

Or, you can cook your own garbanzo beans and use the water to make the rice.

Optional: Add, shallots or onion and yellow bell pepper cut up fine.

Dressing:

You can us a simple olive oil and lemon drizzle.
Or, mix up a batch of Citrus Spring Dressing *(pg 58)*

Tip:

Talk about a salad that packs a great deal of
super foods in it! The almonds add protein,
the chick peas as well have
protein and the broccoli creates an
antioxidant dream come true.

Nutty Arugula Salad

*It's also fun to mix Arugula & spinach for this salad and
feel free to add a bit of avocado.*

Salad Ingredients:

- About 2+ cups organic baby Arugula - cut up
- 1/2+ cups organic sliced almonds
- 2 Tbs Canadian Hemp Hearts
- 6 or 7 chopped up organic sun dried tomatoes

Dressing:

- Organic olive oil
- Organic lemon *(to taste)*
- 1 tsp organic cane, or pinch of Stevia, or a spoonful of honey
- 1/2 green apple or pear cut up
- A pinch of mineral salt

Blended all the dressing ingredients in the Bullet, or food processor.
Pour over the salad just before serving and enjoy!

Tip:

Hemp hearts are a complete protein.
High in minerals and vitamins as well
as calcium and iron. It is wise to keep
a high grade jar of hemp hearts
in your kitchen pantry.

Beets & Peas

Beets were used in ancient Roman times, medicinally and as an aphrodisiac. These facts are backed by science, not just legend.

Why beets?

Beets are an accent root food. There are so many amazing nutrients in beets it is difficult to cover them all. How about potassium, magnesium, iron and phosphorus? A high fiber vegetable is an added plus. High in vitamin A, B, C and folic acid not to mention beta carotene.

Beets also help to purify the blood and are great for the liver. Research shows beets may also help prevent many forms of cancer.

Beets contain a substance named betaine and tryptophan. These both help relax the mind and lower blood pressure. So, when we ask why would we want a beet salad? These are just a few of the answers. Beets can be eaten raw or steamed, hot or cold.

Why Peas?

Green peas area leguminous and have high amounts of vitamins, minerals and are also a good anti-oxidants. Peas have folic acid (Folate is a B complex that is great for your body. It is what they give you when you are pregnant to insure a healthy brain in your child.) Folate also helps to bring down your homocysteine and that equals lower risk of a heart event.

Peas are also a source of K1 and Vitamin A.

Peas are high in Lutein and that is great for your eyes!

You can even gain the benefits of many minerals such as copper, iron, zinc and manganese from peas. Fresh peas are best. I used canned peas in this photo. Please take the time to use fresh if you can!

Why together?
Besides purple and green being my two favorite colors.
These two actually compliment each other nutritionally.
So, don't hesitate to have a colorful plate.

Tip:
Please know that eating beets (especially raw beets) may turn your urine pink for a day or so. Not to panic or worry, it is just this amazing root doing it's job.

Oriental Vegan Delight

Ingredients:

- 2 cups + organic Romaine lettuce cut fine
- 1- 2 cups thinly slice cabbage
- Thinly sliced red onion *(optional)*
- Chopped scallions or green onions with tops
- 2 Tbs slivered almonds
- 1 organic carrot grated fine
- 1 - 2 tsp cilantro chopped fine

Optional:

- Cut up orange section, or cut up half organic pear
- 1 Tbs *(or a little less)* sesame seeds
- 1/4 to 1/2 cup peas *(fresh or organic canned)*
- Top it off with sprouts *(sunflower is pictured)*

Method:

Step 1:   Chop all ingredients, carrots are best grated fine.

Step 2:   Toss all together and drizzle with Peanut Delight Dressing. *(pg 59)*

Note: If you love peas, have more peas, if you love onions have more onions etc.

Tip:

Sunflower seeds and sprouts are packed full of B vitamins, especially folate. Also high amounts of zinc and vitamin E. This hearty sprout can be chopped up in any salad or used as a garnish. In this case, eat your garnish! Boost your healing properties of your salad by using sunflower sprouts.

Healthy Salad Dressings

Basic Healthy Dressing

Ingredients:

- 2 Tbs organic virgin olive oil
- 1/2 organic lemon squeezed *(juice)*
- About 1/4 tsp Stevia *(to taste)*

Method:

I like to put them on the salad and toss the salad.

You may also blend them in a bullet or whisk the ingredients to make a blended dressing.

Z Green Goddess

Ingredients:

- 2 Tbs organic olive oil
- 1 to 2 tsp apple cider vinegar
- 1/2 avocado
- A slice of green pepper
  (can be yellow as well)
- 1/2 ripe peach or about 9 green grapes
- Stevia or honey to taste

Method:

- Put all ingredients into a bullet or blender, blend till smooth.

- Taste... adjust for your perfect Green Goddess!

Spring Citrus

Ingredients:

- 2 Tbs organic olive oil
- 1/2 organic orange
  (leave about 1/4 of the peel on)
- 1 capful apple cider vinegar or
  rice vinegar
- 2 tsp clean water
- 2 tsp organic honey
  (you may also use Xylitol or Stevia)

Optional:

- Small amount of fresh ginger for zing.
- Also try a bit of nutmeg for a change of
  flavor.
- Use peanut oil for a mild taste.

Method:
Blend in a bullet or blender for 30 sec. until desired consistency.

A few tips about Olive Oil:
There is nothing finer than a really good high grade extra virgin organic olive oil. It is filled with antioxidants and omega 3's. There have been many science reports that say *"Do not expose your oil to high heat because it becomes oxidized."* Do your own research and remember to use only fresh oil, as any oil will oxidize with age and that in turn is not good for your body. Oil responsibly.

Peanut Delight

Ingredients:

- 2 Tbs peanut oil or sesame oil
- 2 tsp rice vinegar
- 1 tsp apple cider vinegar
- 1 heaping tsp organic smooth peanut butter
- 1/2 tsp Xylitol or 1 tsp honey *(to taste)*
- 1 Tbs sesame seeds

Optional:

A few drops of Bragg's aminos.
This deepens and darkens the flavor.

Method:

- Whisk all ingredients till smooth and creamy.

- Taste, you may add a bit more vinegar or hone depending if you like sweet or sour.

This recipe is great for a dipping sauce as well.

The measurements above make enough for a large salad. If you have a few people feel free to double the amounts. You can also withhold the sesame seeds and sprinkle them on top of the salad for a nice finish.

South of the Boarder

Ingredients:

- 2 Tbs organic virgin olive oil
- 1 Tbs green salsa
- 1 teaspoon organic cumin
- 1 Tbs cut up cilantro
- 1/2 juiced lime

Method:

- Blend or whisk all ingredients together.

- Taste and add a bit of honey if you like it sweet (or add more cumin or cilantro).

- Adjust to your taste as this *South of the Boarder Dressing* is also great as a side for beans or burritos.

Papaya Delight

Ingredients:

- 1/2 Hawaiian Papaya *(clean out pits)*
- 2 tsp rice vinegar
- 2 Tbs almond Oil
- 1 Tbs coconut or almond milk
- Pinch of salt

Method:

- Blend all in a bullet. *Dressing may be thick so add a tsp of almond or coconut milk.*
- Blend till smooth.
- Drizzle over salad or toss into salad.

This mild dressing is the greatest for your digestion and gives a feeling of being on a tropical island.

Home Made Thousand Island

Ingredients:

- 2 Tbs organic mayonnaise
- 1 - 1/2 Tbs organic ketchup
- 1 - 2 tsp almond milk *(or less)*

Method:

- Blend with a whisk to desired taste and color.

This is a healthy way to have Thousand Island Dressing without the chemicals of store bought dressing.

I love to dip my sweet potato fries in this.

Z Yogurt Sauce

Ingredients:

- 2 heaping Tbs plain yogurt
- 1 Tbs finely grated cucumber
- 1 tsp almond milk
- 1/2 - 1 tsp dill *(fresh or dried, chopped fine)*
- Pinch of mineral salt
- Pinch of Red Top Spike seasoning

Method:

- Place the plain yogurt in a glass or stainless steel bowl.

- Add the dill and the almond milk with a pinch of salt and if you like "spike."

- Mix all ingredients with a spoon or whisk until the consistency you desire.

- This makes a great dressing for greens, a sauce for a sandwich, or as a dipping sauce.

Sometimes, we think of side dishes as add ons.
The truth is, your side dishes and your snacks can be a pivotal point in receiving the nutrition your body needs on a daily basis. Not terribly hungry? Have a healthy snack! It is even fun sometimes to make a meal out of a few snacks. At times, I will make sweet potato fries, have a few stalks of organic celery with organic peanut butter or a Granny Smith apple with peanut or Almond butter and that makes a perfect small meal for me.
How about you?

Healthy Snacks, Sides & Sauces

" It's that time of day, feeling a bit low on energy?
Have a healthy snack! It may also help your glucose to stay
level and energize you. Yes! to a healthy snack."

Cauliflower Mashed Potatoes

Dense nutrition without the starch!

Ingredients:

- 2 cups cauliflower florets & stalk
- Organic butter
- 1/4 cup almond milk *(or less)*
- Pinch of mineral salt

Method:

Step 1: Cut up the cauliflower into chunks.

Step 2: Steam the cauliflower until very soft. Place cauliflower into a blender. *(A bullet blender is best)*

Step 3: About 1/4 cup (or less) almond milk, hemp milk, or milk of your choice. Blend till smooth and either creamy or stiff. Use butter to top it off. Delicious!

TIP: *I agree with Dr. Mercola that cauliflower is a super food and here is some documented proof.*

1. Cauliflower fights cancer. Cauliflower contains sulforaphane, a sulfur compound that has also been shown to kill cancer stem cells, may help prevent and treat prostate cancer. According to the National Cancer Institute: *"Indoles and isothiocyanates have been found to inhibit the development of cancer in several organs in rats and mice, including the bladder, breast, colon, liver, lung, and stomach."*

2. Boost Heart Health. Sulforaphane in cauliflower and other cruciferous vegetables has been found to significantly improve blood pressure and kidney function

3. It's Anti-Inflammatory. You need some level of inflammation in your body to stay healthy. However, it's also possible, and increasingly common, for the inflammatory response to get out of hand. Cauliflower contains a wealth of anti-inflammatory nutrients to help keep inflammation in check, including indole-3-carbinol or I3C, an anti-inflammatory compound that may operate at the genetic level to help prevent the inflammatory responses at its foundational level 5.

4. It's Rich in Vitamins and Minerals. Eating cauliflower regularly is a simple way to get these much-needed nutrients into your body. For instance, one serving of cauliflower contains 77% of the recommended daily value of vitamin C. It's also a good source of vitamin K, protein, thiamin, riboflavin, niacin, magnesium, phosphorus, fiber, vitamin B6, folate, pantothenic acid, potassium, and manganese.

5. Boost Your Brain Health. Cauliflower is a good source of choline, a B vitamin known for its role in brain development. indicating that eating cauliflower may boost cognitive function, and improve learning and memory. It may even diminish age-related memory decline and your brain's vulnerability to toxins during childhood, as well as conferring protection later in life.

6. Detoxification Support. Cauliflower helps your body's ability to detoxify in multiple ways. It contains antioxidants that support Phase 1 detoxification along with sulfur-containing nutrients important for Phase 2 detox activities. The glucosinolates in cauliflower also activate detoxification enzymes.

7. Digestive Benefits. Cauliflower is an important source of dietary fiber and so very good for digestive health.

8. Antioxidants and Phytonutrients Galore. Eating cauliflower is like winning the antioxidant and phytonutrients lottery. It's packed with vitamin C, beta-carotene, kaempferol, quercetin, rutin, cinnamic acid, and much more. Antioxidants are nature's way of providing your cells with adequate defense against attack by reactive oxygen species (ROS).

Cauliflower Rice (Plain & Fancy)

A great and nutritious way to replace a high carb starch with a vegetable!

Ingredients for Plain Cauliflower Rice:

- Raw organic cauliflower

Method:

- Chop in a food processor till it looks like rice! and that is it.
  You can chop by hand, but a processor does the best chopping.
  Enjoy raw, or see below for a fancy side dish.

Ingredients for Fancy Cauliflower Rice:

- 1 - 2 cups cauliflower florets
- 2 Tbs coconut oil
- 1 tsp butter *(if you are not vegan)*
- 1 - 2 Tbs Almond milk
- 1 tsp Pitta Ayurveda Seasoning *(page 156)*

  Optional: 1 Tbs raisins

Method:

Step 1:   Chop the cauliflower in a food processor till it looks like rice!

Step 2:   Place 2 Tbs of coconut oil in a sauce pan on medium heat.

Step 3:   Add the butter and the Cauliflower Rice. Saute for a minute or 2
(at most) and add in the seasoning.

Step 4:   Stir with spatula and add in the almond milk and raisins.

Step 5:   Stir till rice is coated with seasoning. *The almond milk
will absorb almost immediately.*

Step 6:   Remove from heat and serve!

Makes a great healthy snack or side dish.

Plain Cauliflower Rice

Fancy Cauliflower Rice

Peanut Butter & Apple

*This timeless snack may seem simple and yet it packs
super valuable nutrition for the body.*

Granny Smith "green apples" are high in antioxidants and research has shown that green apples may also be instrumental in lowering the risk of many cancers, including lung, colon and liver. Even the *Huffington Post* has reported this great news about Granny Smith Apples.

Organic peanut butter is high in protein, magnesium and potassium which are all good for maintaining normal blood pressure and the healthy fats help to fortify muscles and bones. It also has Vitamin E and B6. There have actually been studies that show people who consume peanuts and peanut butter may actually be helping to decrease the risk of diabetes, heart disease and other age related diseases.

Take a step back in time and enjoy Granny Smith & peanut butter.

1 Tbs peanut butter is great.
1/2 Granny Smith apple is fine for a snack.

*Eating a whole apple would also be good.
"An apple a day with peanut butter
may indeed keep illness away"*

Tip:

Please buy organic peanut
butter with NO sugar added.
Your whole body will say
thank you!

Sweet Potato Fries

Ingredients:

- 1 large well-formed yam or sweet potato - cut up into french fry pieces.
- 1+ Tbs organic olive oil
- Mineral salt to taste *(a pinch or 2)*
- 1/2 tsp - 1 tsp of Red Top Spike seasoning *(optional)*

Method: **Pre heat oven to 350 degrees**

Step 1: Scrub your yam or sweet potato well under cool water.

Step 2: Then slice the yam or sweet potato into about 1/2 inch slices and cut into french fry like pieces as shown in the photo on the opposite page.

Step 3: Place slices in a large bowl and add the olive oil, seasoning, and turn and turn.

Step 4: Place aluminum foil on a cookie sheet and spread the pieces out onto the cookie sheet.

Place in oven for about 30 minutes *(until done)*
Let cool a few minutes.

*I love to eat them with homemade
Thousand Island Dressing. (pg 61)*

Tip: A great spice option is a
pinch of salt, cumin
and chili pepper.
Great for your digestion!

*These are wonderful and nutritious
and a welcomed side dish
or stand alone snack.*

RAW: Susie's Magic Mushrooms!
Very tasty! "Raw food recipe"

I use baby portobellos for this, or whatever mushrooms look freshest!

Ingredients:

- I package of mushrooms *(half a pound)*
- 1 bunch of basil
- 3 - 4 pieces of fresh garlic
- Juice of 2 lemons
  (1 for Basil sauce, 1 for mushrooms)
- 1/2 cup of soaked cashews or pine nuts *(soaked for a few hours)*
- A pinch of Himalayan salt or sea salt
- 1/4 cup of good olive oil

Method:

(soak nuts in water for a few hours prior to making)

Step 1: **Basil Sauce:** Put everything except mushrooms in a blender and blend until creamy.

Step 2: Take stems off mushrooms and put in a large bowl.
Toss with olive oil, *Herbs de Province* and the juice of second lemon.

Step 3: Let marinate an hour or more, then place mushrooms on a cookie sheet.

Step 4: Fill each mushroom cap with the basil sauce.
Eat immediately, but they will be even better the next day... yum!

Susie Fryar, thank you for sharing GlowRawWorld.com

Tip: This is a great way to greet guests. Who doesn't love stuffed mushrooms. And the bonus is, mushrooms strengthen your immune system and help keep your cholesterol under control. The white button mushroom is also very high in Vitamin D, D2, D3. Some say it's as good as taking a supplement.

Take Along Snack: Homemade Kale Chips

Replace those unhealthy potato chips in your pantry with baked kale chips.
Simply slice, drizzle with olive oil, a touch of mineral salt and bake!

Simple Kale Chips Method:

Step 1: Line a cookie sheet with parchment paper and set aside.

Step 2: Wash and chop a desired amount of kale. Make the pieces a bit larger than bite size as they will shrink when drying.

Step 3: Place olive oil and salt in large bowl for coating the kale pieces.

Step 4: Add the kale. After the kale is coated, place on covered cookie sheet and bake at 200 degrees for 25-30 minutes.

(Use a dehydrator at about 150 as directed by dehydrator). Yummy!

Hummus Kale Chips

Method:

Step 1: Take about 1 Tbs of hummus of your choice and add 1 Tbs of water, Almond milk or olive oil, and mix until a thin consistency.

Step 2: Dip or lightly paint the kale pieces with the mixture.

Step 3: Place in oven at 200 degrees and bake until dry and crisp
(approx. 25-30 minutes)
Or, place in dehydrator at 150 until dry and crisp.

Kale is high in fiber, a good source of Vitamin B6, B2, B1, K
(over 600% of RDA on K) Vitamin A, C, E and has folate, calcium,
potassium, niacin, copper and Manganese.
So, if someone asks why eat kale? There's your answer.

A super dense nutrient dark green food, doesn't get better than that.

Tip:

Because kale is high in Vitamin K, please refrain if you are on blood thinners or have had surgery in the last 3 - 6 months. Vitamin K is a coagulant and not for everybody. Eat responsibly.

Fresh Bruschetta Sauce

Ingredients:

- 1 cup diced tomatoes
- 1/2 tsp olive oil
- 1/2 tsp grated garlic
- 1/2 - 1 Tbs grated onions
- 3 - 4 basil leaves cut thin and fine
- 1/2 - 1 tsp Italian seasoning

Method:

Step 1:   Finely chop all ingredients and put into a glass or stainless steel bowl.

Step 2:   Mix gently and there you have it!

The flavor comes out even stronger if you cool it in the fridge for an hour or two.

It's all about the basil! Basil is known as an anti-inflammatory. Some people even use this amazing plant to help with arthritis and IBS. Basil is also great for your digestive tract and has shown benefits in keeping your cardiovascular system in tip-top shape. We all love basil, yes?

Tip:

Tomatoes are an abundant source of antioxidants. Tomato contains large amount of lycopene, an antioxidant that is highly effective in scavenging cancer causing free radicals, as stated by organicfacts. net. Tomatoes are a nightshade and what that means is it can promote inflammation in some people.
So, eat responsibly.

Basic Guacamole

This makes enough for 1 or 2 people max

Ingredients:

- 1 avocado *(pitted)*
- 1/2 lime or lemon
- Pinch of mineral salt

Dress it up:

- 1 Tbs onion chopped fine
- 2 Tbs cilantro chopped *(to your taste)*
- 1 Tbs of Salsa Verde "green salsa"
- Chopped tomato or chili pepper

There are many variations to this great side dish.

Method:

Step 1:   Be sure to chop everything very fine for best results.

Step 2:   I always add a bit of "Salsa Verde" from *Trader Joe's,* It gives a great flavor and makes the guacamole a bit more spreadable.

Step 3:   Mix all ingredients thoroughly.

If you desire a smooth texture just put all ingredients in a bullet.
or small blender and blend to desired consistency.

Tip:
The saying that; "An apple a day keeps the doctor away" also goes for the avocado. Even more so in different ways. The avocado has the "good fats" is heart healthy and great for your brain as well. Any way you slice it, avocado is a food you can eat every day and be better for it.

We all love a nutritionally dense soup.
How awesome that we can get protein,
enzymes, and so many vitamins from a simple soup.
It is so soothing for the body and easy on the digestion.
Soups are great all year round.
Your body will be saying "Thank You" in so many ways.

Soups & 1 Pot Meals

"Love, Love, Love, one pot meals!
A plate of lentils and a salad and we are good to go.
One cup of lentils has 17.9 Grams of protein, 730.6 grams
of potassium and no cholesterol. A dream come true!
Remember your crock pot? It's great for your busy schedules."

Healthy Broccoli Soup

Great as a main course or a side dish.

Ingredients:

- 1/2 yellow onion chopped
- 2 cups broccoli florets with stems - cut up
- 1-2 Tbs *Spike Red Top* Seasoning
- 2 - 4 cups of water
- Dash of Celtic salt
- Optional 1 tsp + chicken flavored or vegetable flavored bouillon

Method:

Step 1: Cut up onion and saute' in organic butter till translucent, about 5 minutes.

Step 2: Add the broccoli and the water, bring to a simmer.

Step 3: Add the Spike and seasonings. Simmer till all is well done and soft.

Step 4: Put into a blender or a Ninja Bullet and process for about a minute, or until desired smoothness is achieved.

This simple soup is packed full of nutrients and will boost your immune system as well.

Broccoli is known to be an anti-cancer, high in folate which has shown to lower your risk of breast cancer. Eating raw and steamed broccoli has also shown to lower the risk of diabetes, heart disease and is an all over super food.

This soup is delicious cold. So no fear, even in the summer you can enjoy "Healthy Broccoli Soup"

Tip: Steam your broccoli to hold in the nutrients. Drinking the water it was steamed in is a healthy boost as well. You will be using most of it to blend your soup into this wonderful meal or side dish.

Yellow Lentil Soup

This is an all time favorite.

Ingredients:

- 16 oz. *(2 cups or 1 package)* organic yellow lentils
- 1/2 – 1 yellow onion
- 1 carrot chopped small *(optional)*
- 1 tsp + Red Top Spike seasoning
- 1 Tbs Dosha Spice *(pg 156)*
- 2 - 4 cups clean water

Method:

Step 1:	Soak yellow lentils in water for a couple of hours.
Step 2:	Drain and use clean water for the soup.
Step 3:	Sauté a yellow onion chopped up fine.
Step 4:	When it is translucent add in the lentils and water.
Step 5:	Add in Spike and turmeric.
Step 6:	Add one heaping tablespoon of the Ayurvedic Dosha spice. *(pg 156)*

Allow to simmer.

Optional: Chop a carrot or two and add to the soup and simmer.
This adds a wonderful sweet taste to your yellow lentil soup.

Tip: Besides having no cholesterol, yellow lentils are heart healthy as they have folate in them. Folate lowers your homocysteine and that, in turn, lowers your risk of heart disease. They have lots of magnesium and that improves blood flow. Lentils even have a low glycemic index and that is great for your blood sugar levels. So, feel free to have this wonderful soup any day or evening.

GG Pearl's & Grandma's Chicken Soup

This soup is an amazing healer. I like to use organic chicken legs as they are highest in vitamin K2, and I do not remove them from the water. I allow them to boil as much as possible as the bone broth has so many healing properties.

Ingredients:

- 1 organic chicken
  (whole, cut-up, or just legs)
- 2 - 3 carrots cut up
- 2 or more celery stalks cut up
- 1 lg onion cut up

- 1 - 2 parsnips cut up
- Salt and pepper to taste
- 'Spike' is great also with a bit of Italian parsley tied at the end
  (optional)

Method:

Step 1: Clean chicken or rinse chicken parts.

Step 2: In a large pot, saute' the chopped onion in a bit of organic butter until the onion is almost clear.

Step 4: Add the chicken and about 6 cups of water to the pot.

Step 5: Add the Spike seasoning.

Cook for about 1 hr. for a whole chicken and about 30 to 40 minutes for chicken parts.

Step 6: Add all the vegetables to the pot.

Simmer for another 30 - 40 min.
And there you have the "no mess way" of preparing this delicious soup.

Note: Prior to adding the vegetables to the pot, some people like to remove the chicken from the pot after it is cooked and take all the meat off the bones, remove all skin, and remove the parsley and discard. Then add the chicken meat back into the pot along with the vegetables, simmer on low until vegetables are tender and serve.

Note 2: I add about 1 tsp chicken bouillon for more flavor.
I use *Better Than Bouillon*, in a jar.

Tip:

This recipe is easily converted into a VEGAN soup just by using tempe or tofu in place of the organic chicken legs.

Vegan Cabbage Soup

(You can also make this a hearty meaty soup by adding 1 lb. stewing meat)

Ingredients:

- 1 cabbage *(center cut out of cabbage)* sliced and cut up
- 1 lb. stewing meat *(optional)*
  If not using meat, use a bit of Worcheshire sauce to replace meat.
- 1 48 oz. can tomato juice
- 1 Lg onion chopped
- 3 Tbs minced parsley
- 1 can (28 oz.) stewed tomatoes

- 1 lemon *(juice of a lemon)*
- 1 clove garlic or a bit of garlic powder *(optional)*
- 5 cups of water
- Sugar or Stevia to taste
- Salt and pepper to taste
- Lemon to taste

(Carrots,Celery, Parsnip are optional)

Method:

Step 1: Saute' onion in a bit of Grapeseed oil or butter.

Step 2: When onion is soft and a bit brown, add the water, tomato juice, parsley, garlic, stewed tomatoes and cabbage.

Let simmer for about 30 minutes to 1 hour.

If you add carrots or other veggies let simmer a full hour.
This soup can simmer for up to 2 hours. (Serve hot or cold)

I prefer to use all stewed tomatoes in this soup and NOT tomato juice.
Try it and see what is best for you. You can also use fresh tomatoes,
probably about 8 large tomatoes will do it.

This recipe was handed down from my mom who was born at the beginning of 1900.

Tip:
Cooked cabbage is high in
antioxidants which include
vitamin A, C and Beta- Carotene,
potassium and is very
low in calories.

Healthy Butternut Squash Soup

Ingredients:

- 2 cups + fresh butternut squash cut into chunks
- 1/2 - 1 yellow onion chopped up
- 1 to 2 tsp *(or less)* Spike Red Top seasoning
- 2 cups water *(less or more depending on how thick you like your soup)*
- Dash of Celtic salt

Optional: Add only about 1/2 tsp Chicken flavored or vegetable flavored bouillon.

Method:

Step 1: Cut up onion and saute' in organic butter *(or coconut oil for a vegan flair)*, until translucent, about 5 minutes.

Step 2: Add the butternut squash and water. Bring to a simmer.

Step 3: Add the Spike and seasonings. Simmer till all is well done and soft.

Step 4: Put into a blender (or a Ninja Bullet) and process for about a minute or until desired smoothness is achieved.

I love to sprinkle a bit of nutmeg and or cinnamon on top.

This simple soup is packed full of nutrients and can soothe your soul.
Great as a main course or a side dish.

Tip:
Beta carotene has been shown to protect against heart disease as well as a deterrent against some cancers and macula degeneration. This isn't the only nutrient or health benefit butternut squash provides. It's rich in potassium, folic acid, magnesium, and omega 3's. You can find this and more info on the web. Butternut squash gets a two thumbs up!

Barley Bake

Ingredients:

- 1 cup pearl barley *(organic if you can find it)*
- 1 yellow or red onion
- 1 Tbs organic butter *(vegan's please use coconut or grapeseed oil)*
- Salt and pepper to taste
- A few shakes of *Red Cap Spike* for deeper flavor
- 1 - 2 cups water

Optional: 1 - 2 stalks celery chopped up.

Method:

Step 1:   Wash barley and drain water.

Step 2:   Cut up onion and saute' in the butter or Grapeseed oil.

Step 3:   When onion is glassy, add the barley and the water.

Simmer about 20 minutes until barley is done.

Barley makes a great side dish to any protein or vegetable dish.
Barley is a low glycemic food and so great with any meal.

Option: To deepen the flavor, use 1/2 - 1 tsp vegetable, chicken, or beef *Better Than Boullion*, or a tsp of Worsheshire sauce.

Tip:

Did you know that barley is a member of the grass family? Barley has been known to help stabilize blood sugar, lower LDL cholesterol and blood pressure. So, it's time to start eating our Barley!

Here in the USA, we think of dinner as our main meal. I am asking that you
think of it as a wonderful *light meal* for the end of a great day.
Did you know that in the U.S. more people have heart events after ingesting a
huge Thanksgiving meal and then going to sleep, than any other time of year?
Your body wants to be well and one way to help our bodies stay well is to eat
responsibly at the evening meal. Too many carbs like bread will raise your
glucose levels as well as sugars, pastas or dense fruits like bananas.
The lighter load we place on our digestive system at night will help the body
to rest well, repair well, wake up invigorated and ready for another wonderful day.

Dinner Anyone?

A time of communing and resting after your long day.
A *lite* dinner is best for your inner and outer wellbeing.
Enjoy a leisurely dinner.

Yummy Casbah Curry

Ingredients:

- 2 Tbs coconut oil *(virgin please)*
- 1/2 yellow onion chopped
- 2 stalks celery chopped
- 1 organic carrot chopped
- 1 cup organic cabbage chopped
- 1 - 1 1/2 cups organic cauliflower chopped
- 1/3 cup yellow pepper chopped
- 2 Tbs honey yogurt
- 1/3 cup cashews
- 1/4 cup organic raisins
- 1 - 2 tsp Ayurvedic curry seasonings *(Pitta or Kapa or both - pg 156)*
- Pinch of mineral salt
- 1 cup almond/coconut milk

Method:

Step 1: Place 2 Tbs coconut oil in a large sauce pan on medium heat.

Step 2: Saute' the onions and carrots until almost tender.

Step 3: Add the rest of the vegetables, including the nuts and the raisins. (Do NOT add the yogurt)

Step 4: Add the almond milk and the Ayurvedic curry seasoning.

Step 5: Stir with a wooden spoon till the sauce becomes thick and vegetables are "al dente."

Step 6: Spoon the honey yogurt over the top and *Yummy Casbah Curry* it is!

Serve with rice, salad or nan.

Casbah Curry in the making

Tip: Curry seasoning is great for your health. Organicfacts.net agrees and says: "Curry powder is a popular spice mix that has a number of valuable health benefits, including the prevention of cancer, protection against heart disease, reduce Alzheimer's disease symptoms, ease pain and inflammation, boost bone health, protect the immune system from bacterial infections, and increase the liver's ability to remove toxins from the body.

Zucchini Pasta

You can use a spirolizer and make the noodles out of Zucchini or use a brown rice gluten free pasta.

Ingredients:

* 1 cup pasta *(either zucchini or brown rice gluten free)*
* 1 - 2 Tbs basil
* 1/2 tsp grated or chopped garlic to taste
* 1 - 2 Tbs good quality olive oil

Optional: Add Parmesan cheese or vegan cheese, if it is your will.

This dish can become a great "raw dish" by using a spirolizer and using raw zucchini as the "pasta." Soften the raw pasta, place in a shallow pan that has hot water in it. Only dip the pasta in to soften a bit if you wish.

Method:

Step 1:	Boil the brown rice pasta till tender.
Step 2:	Grate a clove of garlic.
Step 3:	Chop 3 - 4 good size basil leaves into thin slices.
Step 4:	Place the cooked pasta in a bowl.
Step 5:	Add in the olive oil, the garlic and the basil. Stir till the pasta is well covered.
Step 6:	Top with Parmesan cheese or vegan cheese.

An option is to saute' the garlic pieces, with a bit of chopped spinach for a few minutes before adding to the bowl. (Please use organic butter when sautéing and not the olive oil)

Tip:

Native to India and Asia where it has been cultivated for at least five thousand years, basil is a highly fragrant plant used for seasoning throughout the world

Asparagus Barley Bake
with Mushroom Sauce

Ingredients:

- 1 lb or one package white mushrooms *(organic)*
- 2 Tbs organic butter (*use almond or coconut oil if you are vegan*)
- 1/ large yellow onion cut up
- 1/2 - 1 cup almond or almond/coconut milk

- 1/2 yam or sweet potato
- 3 tsp Bragg's Amino's
- 3 tsp Worsheshire sauce
- 2 - 3 green onions with tops
- 1/2 lb of fresh organic asparagus

Optional: Add cut up zucchini

Method:

Step 1: Wash and prepare mushrooms. *(break the stems off and discard)*

Step 2: Chop up the onion.

Step 3: In a small pot, boil or steam the cut up organic yam.
(I scrub the skin and leave it on)

Step 4: In a larger skillet melt the butter. *(if you are vegan use coconut oil)*

Step 5: Take the onions and about 1/3 of the cut up mushrooms and saute' till soft. Add the seasoning, Bragg's Amino's and A1 or Worsheshire sauce.

Step 6: Add the almond milk and let simmer for a minute or two.

Step 7: Add the cut up and cooked yam.

Take this mixture and put in a blender or food processor for about 30 seconds to a minute. It makes a rich and thick sauce.

Step 8: Place sauce back into pan and add the remainder of mushrooms, asparagus (and zucchini if you choose to add this).

Sautes until the mushrooms and asparagus are soft or to desired state. And there you have it!

Spoon over Barley Bake, Brown Rice, or as seen in the photo a mixture of brown, wild rice and quinoa. Sprinkle chopped green onion on top and serve.

Tip: Did you know asparagus is actually part of the lily family? It is a great plant that helps keep homocysteine in check due to it's high content of B vitamins. It is also high in Potassium, magnesium, iron, manganese, zinc, selenium and iron. All of that in this skinny green vegetable we call asparagus. Please be sure to steam or boil your asparagus for 20 to 30 seconds minimum. Some believe that raw asparagus carries a toxin when eaten raw.

Delicious Quinoa Veggie Combo Meal

Ingredients:

- 2 cups organic Quinoa
  (All ingredients go into pot Raw)
- 4 cup water
  (Aways use purified water please)
- 1 small or 1/2 large onion cut up
- 2 to 3 stalks of celery cut up
- 1 cup + cauliflower florets *cut up small*
- 1 zucchini chopped up

- 1 apple chopped up
- About 1/2 cup raisins
- About 4 sprinkles mineral salt
- Spike - a good amount maybe 2 tsp
- Ayurvedic seasonings *(turmeric and non spicy curry special blend pg 156)*
- 1 Tbs Grapeseed oil or coconut oil if you are going for an exotic taste.

Method:

A crock pot works great and can save you cleaning up a mess in your kitchen.

Step 1: Let it cook until all the liquid is absorbed then let cool a few minutes.

Step 2: Taste...and add what you feel you would like.

This was so delicious and the very first taste was amazing and so nutritious!
A great vegetarian dish for all seasons.
The flavors infuse with each other. Yummmmmm!

Can be cooked in a slow cooker or large pot.

> **Tip:**
>
> This Quinoa is also great cold . With
> the variety of fresh organic veggies
> and low glycemic index,
> this yummy dish is guilt free!

Roasted or Grilled Vegetables
(with Barley bake)

Ingredients:

- Yellow bell pepper *cut into chunks*
- Red bell pepper *cut into chunks*
- Broccoli *cut into chunks*
- Mushrooms *whole to cut or quartered*
- Zucchini *cut into chunks*
- Red Onion *cut into chunks*
- Cherry tomatoes

Whole grilled vegetables are delicious!
Sprinkling a small amount of "Spike" on them will enhance the flavor.

Method:

Step 1:   Cut up vegetables in large chunks and carefully put on the skewers.

Step 2:   Brush lightly with olive oil *(or oil of your choice)*.

Step 3:   Turn frequently.

Place on a grill and watch your veggies so they do not burn.

Optional method:

- Brush vegetables with oil.

Put in a 400 degree oven for 15 - 20 minutes. Check often.

- A bit of Red Top Spike seasoning is a great flavor enhancer.

Enjoy!

Barley Bake see page 92

This seems to be one of my favorite times, indulging my sweet tooth.
How about you? I make an effort to have any glucose raising food early in the day.
However, with the recipes that follow, you are welcome to have them anytime.
Stevia is a supplement for the pancreas and a bit of light fruit is a great way to top off
a wonderful meal. Know that if you eat a bit of protein when you consume a sugar,
it helps to lower the spike of glucose in your bloodstream. A good tip to know.

Sweet Treats

Can you believe it?
Wonderful deserts that you can actually enjoy with
only a natural plant based sweetener.
Now you can enjoy a sweet treat any time of day or night.
I'm so happy about this! How about you?

Organic Raspberry Sorbet

This makes a light and antioxidant rich dessert.

Ingredients:

- 1 cup organic raspberries *(frozen)*
- 1/4 cup almond milk *(I use Casia almond/coconut as it has no caragen in it)*
- 1/2 - 1+ tsp Stevia *(Or less. You can also use Xylitol, or even honey if you are fine with high glycemic index foods.)*

Method:

Step 1:   Place the 3 ingredients in a Ninja Blender or Bullet and blend for about 1 min.

The sorbet will be stiff and you can add a bit more liquid if you need to.

Feel free to double this recipe if you are serving a family or more than 2 people. This is best served fresh.

My favorite topping is a bit of whipped cream. Just a thought!

Tip: Let's talk a bit about this amazing little berry...
Red raspberries contain strong antioxidants such as Vitamin C, quercetin and gallic acid that fight against cancer, heart and circulatory disease and age-related decline. They are high in ellagic acid, a known chemo preventative, and have been shown to have anti-inflammatory properties. *Reported by: berryheath.fst and I so agree.* By using frozen raspberries and a high speed blender you are super sizing the benefits of this wonderful antioxidant.

Z Kitchen Apple Tart

Ingredients:

- 1 cup walnuts
- 2-3 Granny Smith apples
- 1 tsp cinnamon *(to taste)*
- Lemon *(juice 1/4 to 1/2 of a lemon)*
- About 2 Tbs Palm sugar, or 1 Tbs honey or 2 tsp Xylitol
- Organic butter or coconut oil

Optional: Add raisins and nutmeg.
Also, about 9 almonds ground fine will thicken the juices

Crust:

In a Bullet, crush: walnuts, almonds, *(Brazil or your favorite nuts)* until it is the consistency of crushed graham crackers. *(Pecan brings out a heavy rich flavor so use sparingly if you like that).*

Also, if you love the flavor of coconut, you can add a bit of dried coconut. Add just enough coconut oil or organic butter to press the crust into the pie dish you are using.

Fruit Filling:

Step 1: Slice up 2 or 3 "green apples" *(Granny Smith are my favorite).*

Step 2: Core the apples and slice in very thin slices.

Step 3: To thicken the "juices use about 1 Tbs of almond flour or simply put about 9 almonds in a "Bullet" blender for about 30 seconds.

Step 4: Mix this with the apples and it will be like apple pie ...YUM!

Step 5: Sprinkle with honey or sugar.
Add the raisins if you are using raisins and all the spices.

Place in a 350 oven for about 20 minutes or until you have the perfect Apple Tart.
Some like it crispy and nearly raw, and some like it to be like an apple pie. It's your choice.

Tip:

True cinnamon is always the best to use as it may help to regulate blood sugar. Cinnamon is also good for your circulation, your digestion and for your over all health and wellness. So don't be shy, be generous with your cinnamon.

Raw Vegan Key Lime Pie

This is a family favorite. (Raw Vegan) This recipe makes about 10 minis or one pie.

There are many variations of Key Lime pie. I found more than one recipe that seemed good and just needed some tweaking and additional ingredients. So, this is my rendition. Delicious, creamy, light and nutritious.

Crust Ingredients:

- About 1 cup nuts.
  (raw walnuts, slivered almonds, almond meal (flour) you can add coconut flakes if you like.)
- 1 - 2 tsp organic butter or coconut oil *(enough to have the crust stick together)*
- Pinch of salt *(If you want the crust sweet add a bit of Stevia or honey.)*

Method:

Step 1: Put nuts in a blender and mix till the consistency of ground up graham crackers.

Step 2: Add the butter or coconut oil.

*Sometimes I use half butter and half coconut oil.
I also sometime add a bit of dried coconut and blend with
the crust if you love coconut.*

Crust:
- Press the mixture into an 8 inch pie pan, or into 10 cupcake liners about 1 inch mixture in each.
- Place in a hot oven 300 - 350 degrees for about 10 - 15 min. until edges are a bit brown. Set aside to cool.

Filling:

- 2 cups cashews *(soak for about 2-3 hrs)*
- 1 avocado peeled and pitted
- 3/4 + cup Key Lime Juice
- 1 - 2 Tbs lime zest *(to taste)*
- 1 tsp pure vanilla
- 1/3 cup maple syrup *(may use Stevia)*
- 1 - 2 tsp Xylitol
- 1/4 cup liquid virgin coconut oil
- A few shakes of sea or mineral salt

Filling Method:

Step 1:   Rinse and drain the cashews. Place in Bullet or food processor.

Step 2:   Blend for about 30 sec.

Step 3:   Then add all the other filling ingredients and blend till smooth.

Step 4:   Spoon into cooled cup cake liners with crust, or pour into the pie pan.

Step 5:   Grate a bit of lime zest on top. *(grated fine)*

Place in freezer for an hour or two. You can also place in refrigerator for a few hours until filling is cold and stiff. Let stand for a few minutes before serving. Serve cold or cool.

Option:

A dollop of whipped cream is great, or a decoration of chocolate syrup. (Organic vegan chocolate syrup is best)

Tip:
Cashews have many health benefits. They are heart healthy and great for your bones as they are high in magnesium and in copper.
This entire sweet treat is actually in my opinion, very good for your body.

Aztec Chocolate Pudding (Raw Vegan)

Ingredients:

- 1 cup almond milk
- 2 Tbs chia seeds
- 1 Tbs raw cocoa *(heaping if you like dark chocolate)*
- 3/4 tsp cinnamon
- 1/2 tsp cardimon *(unless you love cardimon then you can use a bit more)*
- 1 tsp Stevia *(you can use honey, maple syrup or cane sugar as well)*
  (or a bit less. I use green Stevia as it has more minerals in it - like potassium and magnesium)

Method:

Step 1:   You put all the ingredients into a Bullet or Ninja blender
for about 40 seconds.

Step 2:   Pour into 2 bowls.

Makes 2 (1/2 cup) servings.

Place in refrigerator for about 3 hrs.

I sometime put a bit of Maca Powder *(super food)* and milk thistle *(liver protector)* as you cannot even taste them. I also like to sprinkle some nutmeg on top. I love it best when topped with organic nondairy whipped cream.

Vanilla Nutmeg Pudding
(Raw Vegan)

Ingredients:

- 1 cup almond milk
- 2 Tbs chia seeds
  (you can use a little less for this pudding)
- 1/2 tsp vanilla
- 1/2 tsp ground nutmeg
- 1/4 tsp cinnamon
- 1/4 tsp pumpkin pie spice

- 1/4 tsp cardimon *(unless you love Cardimon then you can use a bit more)*
- 1/2 tsp Stevia *(or a bit less. I use green Stevia as it has more minerals in it - like potassium and magnesium)*
- 1/2 - 1 Tbs Maca super food powder *(optional)*

Great with cut mango mixed in as well

Method:

Step 1: Put all the ingredients into a Bullet or Ninja blender for about 40 seconds.

Step 2: Pour into 2 bowls. Makes 2 (1/2 cup) servings.

Step 3: If it is really thick you can add a bit more almond milk.

I sometimes put a bit of milk thistle *(liver protector)* as you cannot even taste it.
I also like to place it in the refrigerator for about 3 hrs. I love it best when topped with (organic) nondairy whipped cream or a fruit like mango.

Tip: Did you know nutmeg is a brain tonic? It has been used for healing since the time of the Romans. It has properties that can help cleanse the liver and kidneys and even has been know to help with pain. Yes, this little spice packs a big helping hand in natural medicines.

Baked Apples

Baked apples are an all time favorite around my home. Nutritious and delicious.

Ingredients:

- 4 large or medium Granny Smith apples *(cored)*
- 2 - 3 tsp true cinnamon
- 1/2 cup water
- 1 - 2 tsp organic butter

Do not bake with honey, it changes the molecular make up of the honey that no longer gets along with the body.

Option: I use a bit of nutmeg and sometimes pumpkin pie spice.

Method:

Step 1: Place the water on the bottom of the pan. I use a square Pyrex pan.

Step 2: Place the 4 apples on the Pyrex pan and put the tab of butter in each cored apple.

Step 3: Sprinkle the cinnamon and other spices.

Place them into a preheated oven of 350 degrees.
Bake about 25 - 35 minutes. Allow to cool a bit and enjoy.

Tip: Talk about an apple that is high in fiber and vitamins! Granny Smith fits the bill. They also have Quercetin which has shown promise in helping the brain and fights free radicals.
Yes! Granny Smith is the apple of choice!

Organic Pumpkin Pie

A holiday favorite and so healthy you can have it for breakfast as well.

Crust:

- About 1 cup of sliced raw almonds *(you can also add some walnuts for a richer flavor)*
- Put in a Bullet and grind *(I used Trader Joe's slivered raw almonds)*
- A small amount of pure maple syrup, about 1/2 Tbs if you want a sweet crust. Or, a bit of organic Stevia If you like.

Optional: About 1 Tbs dried coconut
1 - 2 tsp organic butter *(just enough to make it stick together)*

You can use a small amount of coconut oil but, I find the taste of organic butter makes it seem richer.

(The Bullet makes the perfect texture with the flat blade,
but you could use a processor or blender on low)

Crust Method:

Step 1:   Put the sliced almonds and coconut in blender.
Blend for a few seconds.

Step 2:   Then put the mixture in a bowl and add a bit of melted butter and smash with a spoon.

Step 3:   Add a bit of maple or Stevia to taste.

Step 4:   Butter the sides and bottom of the pie pan, spread the mixture evenly, smushing it with your hand until it looks like the perfect crust. *(you are welcome to use the bottom of a glass as well)*

Step 5:   Add some almond flour if you want a more thicker crust.

Step 6:   Make the crust and set aside.

Heat in a 375 degree oven for about 10 minutes if you want a crispier crust.
Allow it to cool before pouring the filling in.

Pie Filling:

- One can organic pie filling *(Trader Joe's is my favorite if you have one near by)*
- 1¼ cup Almond Milk *(Recipe for almond milk from scratch is in the sauce section)*
- 2 eggs *(organic free range please)*
- 1/2 cup brown sugar *(or substitute with organic maple syrup-to taste. Less than 1/2 cup usually does it. Or, use Stevia for low or no glycemic index)*
- 1/4 tsp salt
- 1-2 Tbs pumpkin pie spice
- I usually add about 1/2 Tbs of cinnamon and a bit of nutmeg as well.

Pour the filling into the pie crust and bake at 375 for 45 - 50 min.
The pumpkin pie may still be a firm liquid in the middle. It becomes more like a pie as it cools. Be sure a tooth pick comes out dry about 2 inches from pie rim. Enjoy this delicious treat.

OPTION:

Pumpkin from scratch: Cut and scrape a pumpkin. Cut into pieces. Bake on a baking sheet at 375 - 400 degrees for about 45 min. When the pumpkin is soft, peel the skin off and blend it. Put in a small bit of water to make a puree.

Now your talking! Worried about not being able to consume enough greens or super foods? Here is your answer. You can pack a great amount of nutritionally dense ingredients into your green smoothie. You can add some milk thistle, nettle root or chaga as well. Enjoy a green drink anytime! Add a bit of crushed ice and it is a great summer cooler. May I share a secret with you? I don't like raw kale, but a hand full of raw kale in my green drink tastes awesome! Why? Because I cannot even taste the kale! Get your "Raw On" by juicing or better yet, blending!

Green Drinks

Z Wellness Green Drink

Ingredients:

- 1 handful *(or about 1 - 2 cups)* spinach *(organic please)*
- 1/2 cup frozen red organic grapes *(enough to cover blades)*
- 1/ + Tbs fresh organic wheat grass
- 1/2 lime *(with some zest left on it)*
- 1 orange *(organic cut up and some zest left on it)*
- 1 organic Granny Smith apple cut *(leave skin and pits on as well)*
- 1 cup pineapple *(or 100% pineapple juice NOT from concentrate!)*
- Fresh ginger *(about 1-2 inches with skin removed)*

Method:

Step 1:   Place the grapes in the blender first, then all the cut up vegetables and fruits.

Step 2:   Blend on high for at least 2 min.

Step 3:   Add about 1 cup crushed ice.
Add a bit of water if it seems to be to thick.

Step 4:   You can also throw in a bit of kale and flaxseed if you like.

There is a restaurant called "Greens and Proteins"
that make something similar" It's yummy!

Tip: A green drink is the best way to
get your 10 helpings of fruits and
vegetables. It is so yummy and so
good for every part of your body.
Green drinks with fruit in them
tend to be a bit high in natural
sugar so the best time of day to
enjoy your green drink— in my
opinion— is before 2 pm.

The Beet Goes On!

Blood pressure tonic

Ingredients:

- 2 whole organic beets cut up
- 3 - 4 stalks of organic raw dandelion greens *(very bitter, use with caution)*
- 1 cup organic raw spinach
- 1/2 cup pineapple or fresh pineapple juice
- About 1 cup frozen grapes, on bottom *(Just enough to almost cover blade)*
- 1 organic Granny Smith apple
- 1/4 organic lime
- Crushed ice
- May need about 1/2 - 1 cup water

Method:

Step 1:   Place the frozen grapes in the blender first.

Step 2:   Then add the ice and all the vegetables.

Step 3:   Blend for at least 1 - 2 minutes, until your desired smoothness occurs.

If this mixture is too thick feel free to add a bit of water or even a bit of almond milk.

Tip:
We all know that beets are
great for you. Just remember
not to panic when your urine
is pink for a day or two.

Protein Smoothie

Almond milk, Peanut Butter, Raw Cocoa

Ingredients:

- 1 cup organic almond/coconut milk
- 1/2 - 1 Tbs organic peanut butter
- 9 - 10 raw almonds
- 1/2 banana
- 1/2 cup crushed ice

*To make this a chocolate/peanut butter smoothie add
1 - 2 tsp raw organic cocoa*

Sprinkle Nutmeg on top and YUMMM!

If you want to make this super sweet,
add a bit of organic honey, Stevia or Xylitol.

The almonds give you protein and help to "un-spike" the sugar of the banana.
The banana is loaded with fiber and potassium.

*If you have "shakeology protein powder"
this becomes totally super charged!*

Feel free to sprinkle true cinnamon on top as well.

Tip:
The peanuts and almonds are high in the good fats and
also high in protein. So, this make a great snack as well.
The nutmeg on top adds a great taste! I have also used
Pumpkin Pie Spice and find it really delicious as well.

Apple/Celery Juiced

Simple and great for the blood

Ingredients:

- 1 green apple cut up *(pits and all)*
- 3 stalks of organic celery

This is a great pick me up and a simple "juice" you can make at home. Be sure to save all the fiber and use in soup or another blended green drink, that day.

Method:

This drink is best juiced and not blended.
However, if you choose to blend, add crushed ice and blend at least 2 minutes.

Use the freshest celery and green apples you can find and drink immediately for the most absorbable nutrients.

Amounts above are for 1 person.

Tip:
Celery is a strange vegetable. First of all, it has "negative calories" and that means it takes more calorie "energy" for the body to digest it that it has to begin with. It also has a calming effect on the body and has been found to help lower blood pressure. It is also high in B vitamins and that is great for your body and your brain. Be sure to juice the leaves as well, as they are high in Vitamin A and that is great for your eyes and so much more. You can enjoy celery juice anytime day or night.

Immune Boost

Orange, Green Apple, Carrot, Lime, Lemon and Ginger

Ingredients

- 1 organic Granny Smith apple *(peel, seeds and all)*
- 2 - 3 organic oranges
  (take the peal off of 1 or 2 and leave some peel on the last orange)
- 2 organic carrots
- Fresh organic ginger to taste about 1 - 2 inches of root, peal outer skin
- 1/2 lemon or lime with a bit of zest left on
- About 1/4 - 1/2 cup water or crushed ice if you need more liquid

Optional: *To super charge this immune booster add 1 tsp of turmeric.*

Method:

You can use frozen grapes if you like as a base for this power packed smoothie.

- Blending is better than juicing as you retain all the natural fiber of the fruits.

- Juicing is fine if you do not have a high speed blender or Nutri Bullet.

Tip: Why do we want to leave some orange peel on? Because science has found that the skin of an orange is very anti-cancer and we all like that idea I am sure. Make sure your orange is organic in order to make the most of these benefits.

Very Berry Antioxidant

*The variety of colors are a reflection of the berries
that are used in your smoothie.*

Ingredients:

- 1/2 cup organic red raspberries
- 1/2 cup organic blueberries
- 1 cup fresh pineapple juice, or orange juice
- About 1/2 cup frozen grapes
- Crushed ice

Optional: Honey, Stevia or Xylitol to taste

*A handful of organic spinach wouldn't hurt and it adds
tons of iron to this very berry smoothie.*

Method:

Step 1:   Place frozen grapes on bottom.

Step 2:   Add berries.

Step 3:   Add juice.

Step 4:   Add ice.

Step 5:   Blend in a Ninja bullet or high speed blender.

Optional: Feel free to add a bit of spinach, almond milk
or a bit of water if needed.

Peppermint 138
Hibiscus 140
Echinacea 142
Nettle Root 144
Bergamot 146
Ginger 148
Green Tea 150

Throughout history, teas have been used as medicine. As far back as 500 BC.
The original medicine was in tea form. They would dry the plants
and then seep them to extract the medical qualities.
We are just recently beginning to understand and honor medicinal teas.
Make no mistake, it is powerful medicine. So, tea responsibly.
Research what teas are best suited for you. In this medicinal tea chapter you can
gain what I call *Tea Wisdom* and use it to enhance your Vibrant Health.
Enjoy!

Medicinal Teas

Tea is medicine... and very powerful as well!
From taming blood sugar to settling your tummy.
Tea is a wonderful way to love yourself from the inside out.

Peppermint

Peppermint tea is a delicious and refreshing way to boost your overall health in a number of ways, due to its ability to improve digestion, reduce pain, eliminate inflammation, relax the body and mind, cure bad breath, aids in weight loss and boosts the immune system.

It's impact on the digestive system is considerable, and its base element of menthol is perhaps the most valuable part of it's organic structure.

The mentholated flavor is very appealing to many people, making this one of the more popular tea varieties in the world. Tea is known to be soothing, sure, but what else does this widely available tea have for our bodies in terms of benefits? Let's explore some of those other medicinal applications of peppermint tea below.

Health Benefits of Peppermint Tea.

Report from organicfacts.net:

Fever Reducer: When we think of the sharp, cool effect of menthol, we don't necessarily think of a hot cup of tea, but peppermint tea has menthol as a main component, so, drinking the tea can cause external sweating, while the menthol cools down your body inside. This essentially "breaks" a fever, and can reduce the associated inflammation and discomfort.

Digestive Health: Peppermint oil and peppermint tea have been used for thousands of years to sort out a variety of digestive and gastrointestinal conditions. Archaeological evidence actually shows peppermint being used as far back as 10,000 years ago as a dietary supplement. Peppermint tea is considered a carminative, meaning that it helps to move gas through the body as it accumulates, rather than causing bloating, cramping, and stomach discomfort. The tea also stimulates bile flow to increase the rate and efficiency of digestion and promote healthy bowel movements. It is calming on the digestive system so can help ease IBS (irritable bowel syndrome) gas and discomfort.

Nausea and Vomiting: When it comes to being sick, few things are as unpleasant as being nauseous or vomiting. Peppermint tea is antispasmodic, so it reduces the chances of vomiting and nausea, even in cases of motion sickness on a boat or a plane. It also reduces the stomach aches and queasiness associated with motion sickness, and it's anti-inflammatory qualities can return your stomach to normal.

Respiratory Issues: As an antispasmodic, it can also relieve you of that irritating sensation that makes you want to cough, thereby exacerbating your respiratory condition. By relaxing the muscles of the throat and chest, you can eliminate that aspect of cold and flu symptoms.

Immune System: Peppermint tea has known antibacterial properties, which are the cause of so many illnesses, including fevers, coughs, and colds. Not only can drinking this

delicious tea help you treat the symptoms of being ill, it can also prevent your body from getting sick in the first place! There are also trace elements of vitamin B, potassium, antioxidants and calcium, which can help your body uptake nutrients to fight off illness and perform necessary function to keep your body working in a healthy way.

Bad Breath: The strong, mentholated flavor and antibacterial quality of peppermint tea make it an ideal way of improving your breath. The antibacterial element kills the germs that can lead to halitosis, while the menthol overwhelms the foul smell and leaves your breath fresh and clean!

Weight Loss: The aroma of peppermint oil and some of its organic components can actually eliminate the appetite, so smelling this substance can help reduce overeating, and subsequently, obesity!

Stress Levels: The natural sedative and antispasmodic nature of menthol makes it very good at relieving mental stress. The anti-inflammatory nature can reduce blood pressure and body temperature, and allow you to unwind and relax, letting your cares melt away.

A Few Words of Caution: It is a powerful type of tea, and although it does have the wide range of health benefits explained above, there are still some possible side effects. The menthol can act as an allergen to some people, and can cause heartburn in others. Both of the reactions are typically mild, but consulting a doctor about possible allergies is always a good idea. Besides that, grab some peppermint leaves and get brewing!

Hibiscus

AHHH Hibiscus:
Hibiscus, the beautiful red flower that has been used for centuries as an excellent medicinal tea. In the far reaches of the globe, this flower when dried, has been known for its health properties, specifically for those looking to support cardiovascular health. It is refreshing with a slight sour taste.

GiaHerbs.com states: *In Egypt and Sudan, Hibiscus is used to help maintain a normal body temperature, support heart health, and encourage fluid balance.

North Africans have used Hibiscus internally for supporting upper respiratory health including the throat and also use it topically to support skin health.

In Europe, Hibiscus has been employed to support upper respiratory health, alleviate occasional constipation, and promote proper circulation.

*It is commonly used in combination with lemon balm and St. John's Wort for restlessness and occasional difficulty falling asleep.

Hibiscus is traditionally used for supporting normal blood pressure maintenance.

How to use:

For cholesterol maintenance: One cup of Hibiscus tea 2x daily, or 100 mg of standardized extract 2x daily.

For blood pressure maintenance: One cup of Hibiscus tea 2x daily or dried powdered Hibiscus extract providing 250 mg anthocyanins per day.*

Approximately 15-30 percent of the Hibiscus plant is made up of plant acids, including citric acid, malic acid, tartaric acid and allo-hydroxycitric acid lactone — i.e. Hibiscus acid, which is unique to Hibiscus.

There have been many studies on Hibiscus and it's beneficial effects on blood pressure and cholesterol.

Echinacea

This lovely flowering plant is probably the pinnacle of herbal preventatives.

Echinacea is not only anti-bacterial—but it stimulates the body's immune system to fight off bacterial and viral attacks. The medicinal properties are in the leaves and the purple flowers.

Growing it: Echinacea is also known as the "purple cone flower." The plant has deep tap-roots and is somewhat drought resistant. It is a perennial.

Sow seeds outdoors in the early spring before the last frost. These plants like full sun and they don't like too much moisture.

Echinacea tea can help to:

- Enhance the immune system
- Reduce inflammation
- Shorten illness time for sufferers of the common cold
- Relieve pain
- Provide antioxidant effects

Archaeologists have found evidence that Native Americans may have used Echinacea for more than 400 years to treat infections and wounds, and as a general "cure-all." Throughout history people have used Echinacea to treat scarlet fever, syphilis,
malaria, blood poisoning, and diphtheria.

Echinacea is a "short term" tea. Best to drink for about 7 days max and then take a break for a week or so. Take when your immune system needs a boost.

Tip: The University of Maryland Medical Center says: "People with tuberculosis, leukemia, diabetes, connective tissue disorders, multiple sclerosis, HIV or AIDS, any autoimmune diseases, or possibly liver disorders should not take Echinacea. There is some concern that it may reduce the effectiveness of medications that suppress the immune system. For this reason, people receiving organ transplants who must take immuno-suppressent medications should avoid this herbal tea.

Nettle

livestrong.com and Sheila Z

What Is Nettle Tea?

In one of those strange-but-true twists of nature, it turns out that the plant that can cause you so much harm could be the very solution to treating your problems. The stinging nettle, *(Latin name, Urtica dioica)*, has been used medicinally since at least 3 B.C. In medieval times, it was used to treat pain in joints, as well as act as a diuretic. Today, nettle root is used to treat urinary problems associated with an enlarged prostate *(benign prostatic hyperplasia)*, urinary tract infections and hay fever. Nettle leaf, meanwhile, is most commonly used to treat pain, osteoarthritis, allergies and hay fever. The leaves and stems can be eaten in a salad, cooked into soup or made into a tea, but the nettle root is more likely to be extracted with alcohol to make a tincture, dried and taken in capsules, or dried and made into a tea. The plant has few known side effects, but as with any medicinal preparation, you may want to consult a health care practitioner before adding nettles to your diet or treatment plan.

Nettle Tea Benefits

Nettle tea affects the kidneys directly. *"Nettle is a diuretic. It increases urine output and removal of uric acid (under physician supervision). Thus, it can be useful for edema, inflammatory arthritis or gout,"* says naturopath Dr. Robert Kachko, ND, LAC. Studies show that by combining nettle with saw palmetto, patients can find relief from urinary problems. In addition to affecting the kidneys, *"nettle has many constituents and is considered one of our most nutritive herbs, we call it a 'trophorestorative' for this reason,"* says Dr. Kachko. *"Its main constituents are flavonoids (quercetin, kaempferol), carotenoids, Vitamin Cup, Vitamin B, Vitamin K1, triterpenes, sterols and minerals."* Ten grams of nettle contains 290 milligrams of calcium and 86 milligrams of magnesium. In comparison, 10 grams of raw spinach contains 10 milligrams of calcium and 8 milligrams of magnesium.

- Nettle tea has also been used for hay fever "Allergies."
- Nettle tea is known to improve kidney function.
- And is a great addition to your medicinal arsenal.

Tip: Buy your nettle from an
herb store as the quality and
potency will be far superior
than a store bought tea.

Bergamot

livestrong.com and Sheila Z

Bergamot, be it from the bergamot orange or from the unrelated herb known as wild bergamot, offers many health benefits. Though the plants come from different families and species, they have one thing in common: their distinctive aroma. They have a pleasant orange-blossom fragrance that, *(studies have shown),* calm anxiety and depression and aid in digestive ailments.

International Journal of Aromatherapy published a study in 2004 that showed a marked improvement in alleviating anxiety and depression in 32 subjects. So, sipping Earl Grey tea and breathing in that fabulous aroma is a good way to calm your mind at the end of a hectic day.

Bergamot is a powerful anti-microbial, anti-oxidant, and improves digestion.

The *Journal of Applied Microbiology* published a study in 2007 that identified bergamot as a natural anti-microbial. This explains why Native Americans and naturopaths worldwide have used it to treat urinary tract infections and yeast infections, though no studies have proven it effective.

Tip: It turns out that bergamot juice (as opposed to the peel used in Earl Grey tea) contains exceptionally large amounts of several unique polyphenols. And when that juice is extracted, concentrated, and standardized in tablet form, it dramatically lowers triglycerides and LDL cholesterol, raises protective HDL cholesterol, helps control blood sugar and improves overall arterial function and cardiovascular health, as stated by Dr. Whitaker.com

Ginger

Ginger excerpt form Anatomy of Healing and Wellness

This homely root is an ingredient in many natural cough, cold, and nausea treatments. Instead of giving your child ginger-ale when they are suffering from an upset stomach *(with all of the high fructose corn syrup and artificial flavors that come in it)* brew up a nice cup of ginger tea, sweetened with honey for a real dose of soothing ginger!

Growing it: Ginger is a tropical plant that is apparently not difficult to grow indoors. It requires excellent soil, warmth, humidity, and filtered sunlight.

Caution: It's not recommended to exceed 4 grams of ginger per day as components in the herb can cause irritation of the mouth, heartburn and diarrhea if taken in excess. Honey-ginger cough syrup can also be the basis for a nighttime hot toddy.

Ginger tea can be used to:

- Reduce nausea
- Prevent or treat motion sickness
- Warm the body of someone suffering from chills
- Induce sweating to break a fever
- Soothe a sore throat

Tip: Ginger has so many health benefits it may be difficult to list them all. Let's start with this amazing plant is very good for your tummy. It can soothe nausea or other ailments you may be experiencing in your stomach. It is very anti-cancer, so we all could benefit by having a bit of ginger tea. There is research being done with ginger and ovarian cancer with great promise. Ginger has even been shown to work on migraine headaches. Use organic fresh ginger whenever possible for the strongest medicinal benefits.

Green Tea is full of plant antioxidants known as catechins, a compound known to many functions in the body. One of the greatest assets is liver function. Green Tea is delicious, it's also a great way to improve your overall diet. Green Tea does have caffeine in it, so consult your health professional before using Green Tea.

Excerpt from "Anatomy of Healing and Wellness"

Green tea retains maximum amount of antioxidants and poly-phenols—the substances that give green tea its many benefits. Some of these benefits are still being debated, so please, do your own research if you want to use green tea for medicinal purposes.

- **Weight Loss:** The polyphenol found in green tea works to help your metabolism, also intensify levels of fat oxidation.

- **Diabetes:** Green tea apparently helps to regulate glucose levels, slowing the rise of blood sugar after eating. This can prevent high insulin spikes and result in fat storage.

- **Heart Disease:** Scientists think, green tea works on the lining of blood vessels, helping keep them stay relaxed and better able to withstand changes in blood pressure.

- **Esophageal Cancer:** It can reduce the risk of esophageal cancer, and it is also widely thought to kill cancer cells in general without damaging the healthy tissue around them.

- **Cholesterol:** Green tea reduces bad cholesterol in the blood and improves the ratio of good cholesterol to bad cholesterol.

- **Alzheimer's and Parkinson's:** It is said to delay the deterioration caused by Alzheimer's and Parkinson's. Studies carried out on mice showed that green tea protected brain cells from dying and restored damaged brain cells.

- **Tooth Decay:** Studies suggests that the chemical antioxidant "catechin" in tea can destroy bacteria and viruses that cause throat infections, dental cavities and other dental conditions.

- **Blood Pressure:** Regular consumption of green tea is thought to reduce the risk of high blood pressure.

- **Depression:** Theanine is an amino acid naturally found in tea leaves. It is this substance that is thought to provide a relaxing and tranquilizing effect and be a great benefit to tea drinkers.

- **Anti-viral and Anti-bacterial:** Tea catechins are strong antibacterial and anti-viral agents. In some studies green tea has been shown to inhibit the spread of many diseases.

- **Skin care:** Green tea can apparently also help with wrinkles and the signs of aging; this is because of its antioxidant and anti-inflammatory activities. Both animal and human studies have demonstrated that green tea applied topically can reduce sun damage.

Some information sourced from www.lifehack.org

Herbs and spices have always been used as medicine. Even the first Pharaohs in Egypt used herbs to soothe and cure ailments. We live in a time when we are returning to our plants and realize that every plant on this earth has a purpose—a healing to wellness purpose. It is wonderful we can incorporate these healing herbs and spices into our daily foods and benefit from their ancient goodness.

Medicinal Herbs

Turmeric

(Excerpt form Anatomy of Healing and Wellness)

Curcumin, *(a substance in Turmeric),* may help to reduce inflammation. Several studies suggest that it might ease symptoms of osteoarthritis and rheumatoid arthritis, like pain and inflammation.

Other compounds in Turmeric might also be medicinal. In lab tests, Curcumin seems to block the growth of certain kinds of tumors. Other preliminary lab studies suggest that Curcumin (or Turmeric) might protect against types of skin diseases, Alzheimer's disease, colitis, stomach ulcers, and high cholesterol.

Based on these studies, Turmeric and Curcumin might also help treat:

- Upset stomach
- Scabies
- Diabetes
- HIV
- Uveitis
- Viral infections

It is also used as a remedy for digestive problems such as:

- Irritable bowel syndrome (IBS)
- Colitis
- Crohn's disease
- And illnesses caused by toxins from parasites and bacteria

No wonder some people refer to Turmeric as the "wonder spice."

According to Web MD, Turmeric is also used for many ailments such as:

- Headaches
- Lupus
- Worms
- Urinary inflammation
- Skin sores
- Infected wounds
- Skin inflammation from radiation treatment
- Fatigue and recovery from surgery
- Liver problems

Tip:

If you are pregnant do NOT take turmeric. Also, beware if you have any kidney, gallbladder disease, bleeding challenges, immunity problems or diabetes.
Check with your physician.

Ayurvedic Dosha Herbs

Ayurveda, is a 5,000 year old wisdom bringing balance to
the Body, Mind and Spirit.
Maximizing digestion and bringing about a blissful fulfilled life.

Below are the amazing creations by Chef Johnny Brannigan of the
3 Dosha Herb Blends: Pita, Kapha & Vata. All organic!

*These are my personal favorites,
I use them in many of my soups, and veggie dishes.*

Pita:
Balanced by cool dry food. Bitter, sweet and astringent.
Ingredients: Coriander, fennel, cardamom, turmeric, cumin and love.

Kapa:
Balanced by spicy and crunchy food. Pungent, bitter and astringent.
Ingredients: Ginger, cumin, coriander, mustard seed, cayenne pepper and love.

Vata:
Balanced by warm and unctuous food. Sweet like fennel,
sour like sauerkraut and salty like salt.
Ingredients: Fennel, coriander, cumin, ginger, turmeric, basil, asafetida,
salt, coconut sugar and love.

Tip:

Internationally renowned chef Johnny Brannigan has been endorsed by *Deepak Chopra* and these amazing herbs are a compliment to many dishes. You can order these herbs directly from the vedicchef.com web site.

Johnny Brannigan
www.vedicchef.com

SPICE WISDOM
Organic
Vata Seasoning
SPICE WISDOM
Organic
Vata Seasoning
SPICE WISDOM
Organic
Kapha Seasoning

Cinnamon

Cinnamon doesn't just smell like a holiday, it is anti-bacterial, antiviral, and anti-fungal, making it an excellent all-around remedy for whatever ails you. Cinnamon is a wonderful source of immune-boosting antioxidants.

According to a study by Dr. Bryan Raudenbush, Director of Undergraduate Research and Associate Professor of Psychology at Wheeling Jesuit University in Wheeling, *"Cinnamon may keep you more alert and decrease your frustration when you are behind the wheel."*

Anti-oxidant: Cinnamon is one of the top 7 anti-oxidants in the world. The suggestion is that anti-oxidants reduce the formation of "free radicals" that cause cancer. This study found cinnamon has sufficient anti-oxidant properties and makes for improved food palatability. A detailed Indian study also found potential anti-microbial and antioxidant properties of the volatile oils and oleo resins of cinnamon leaf and bark.

So, consider anti-oxidants as good for your whole body, repairing damage to virtually all parts of your body from skin to organs. Just 6 gr. (about 1 tsp) of cinnamon may also help to level out your blood sugar. Cinnamon also helps in acting as an anti-clotting agent, especially for those suffering from heart disease. Care must be taken NOT to take Cinnamon with other blood-thinning medications. The main ingredient that causes your blood to thin is Coumarin, which is present in high doses in Cassia Cinnamon (4%) but not in Ceylon Cinnamon (0.04%). However, Coumarin causes liver damage. So, taking Cassia Cinnamon for weight loss may end up causing liver damage. This article cites Dr. Greenburg of Tufts University as saying it holds promising possibilities for weight loss.

Cinnamon tea can be used to:
- Increase blood flow and improve circulation
- Soothe a sore throat
- Ease stomach discomfort, bloating
- Reduce nausea
- Reduce cold symptoms
- Warm the body of someone suffering gas and indigestion from chills

Nutrients: One teaspoon of Cinnamon Powder (a realistic dose) has 0.33mg (16% DV) Manganese, 0.76 mg (4% DV) Iron, 24.56 mg (2% DV) Calcium. Manganese apparently works as an enzyme activator and plays an important role in building good structure and bone metabolism. According to WebMD: Manganese is therefore useful for weak bones (osteoporosis), a type of "tired blood" (anemia), and symptoms of premenstrual syndrome (PMS).

Tip:
Just 6 gr (1 tsp) of cinnamon can help to regulate your blood sugar. It also makes a great bedtime tea. Try it!

Coriander

Coriander comes from the seeds of the cilantro plant, but they have a very different flavor. Coriander has been around since 5000 BC. Used by the Egyptians and the Romans medicinally and for flavoring.

My research agrees with the information found on Web MD:
Coriander is used for digestion problems including:

- Upset stomach
- Loss of appetite
- Hernia
- Nausea
- Diarrhea
- Bowel spasms
- Intestinal gas

It is also used to treat measles, hemorrhoids, tooth aches, worms, and joint pain, as well as infections caused by bacteria and fungus.

Some breast-feeding women use Coriander to increase milk flow. In foods, coriander is used as a culinary spice and to prevent food poisoning. In manufacturing, coriander is used as a flavoring agent in medicines and tobacco and as a fragrance in cosmetics and soaps.

I also agree with organic facts.net. Cineole, one of the 11 components of the essential oils, and linoleic acid, are both present in coriander, and they possess anti rheumatic and anti-arthritic properties. They help to reduce the swelling that is caused by these two conditions. For other swelling conditions, such as swelling due to kidney malfunction or anemia, it is also seen to be effective—to some extent—because some of the components in coriander help the induce urination and the release of excess water from the body. The reduction in skin inflammation can lead to increased functioning, a reduction in discomfort, and an improvement in skin appearance.

Coriander is a small seed like herb. Do not let its size fool you, it is packed full of vitamins and minerals. It is particularly rich in Vitamins A and K, and also Vitamins B, C and E.

As for the mineral content, coriander has an amazing amount of potassium and is also a good source of calcium, magnesium and phosphorous. So, don't be shy when it comes to using this herb in your favorite dishes.

Cumin

The health benefits of Cumin include its ability to aid in:

- Digestion
- Improve immunity and treat piles
- Insomnia
- Respiratory disorders
- Asthma
- Bronchitis
- Common cold
- Lactation
- Anemia
- Skin disorders
- Boils and cancer

Many of you might remember having hated those curries and soups which had roasted, or fried cumin seeds in them when you were kids, because they looked like small black insects. However, you probably liked the taste. So, your mother might have removed these flavorful parts before she served you the food. That was Cumin!

Cumin, *(scientifically known as Cuminum Cyminum),* belongs to the family Apiaceae, and is extensively used in culinary practices of the Indian sub-continent and some other Asian, African and Latin American countries as a condiment or spice. Cumin can be beneficial in helping to alleviate some of the most dangerous diseases, and is generally consider a boost for overall health.

Diabetes: Although research is still ongoing, early studies report that cumin, among a number of other spices, can have a powerful effect in preventing diabetes by reducing the chances of hypoglycemia. The animals that were tested, showed a sharp decline in hypoglycemia when fed cumin seeds in their diet.

Bronchitis: The presence of caffeine *(the stimulating agent),* and the richly aromatic essential oils *(the disinfectants)* make cumin an ideal anti-congestive combination for those suffering from respiratory disorders such as asthma and bronchitis. It acts as an expectorant.

Skin Disorders: Almost everyone knows that Vitamin-E is good for the maintenance of skin and the prevention of premature aging symptoms. It keeps the skin young and glowing. This Vitamin is also present in abundance in cumin. The essential oils present in cumin have disinfectant and anti-fungal properties.
Is Cumin the Same As Curcumin? (NO).

Cayenne Pepper

(Excerpt from Anatomy of Healing and Wellness)

Health benefits of cayenne peppers:

Although inherently hot and intolerable, even in small amounts, cayenne is one of the health-benefiting spice items packed with minerals, vitamins and certain phyto-nutrients.

It is no wonder this wonderful spice has found a place in modern, as well as in traditional medicines for its disease preventing and health promoting properties. Cayenne contains the health-benefiting alkaloid compound—capsaicin, which gives the strong, spicy, pungent character. Early laboratory studies (on experimental mammals) suggest that capsaicin has anti-bacterial, anti-carcinogenic, analgesic and anti diabetic properties. When used judiciously, it was also found to reduce triglycerides and LDL cholesterol levels in obese individuals.

Fresh cayenne peppers, (red or green) are rich source of Vitamin Cup. 100g fresh chilies provide about 76.4 mg or about 127% of RDA of this Vitamin. Vitamin C is a potent water soluble antioxidant. It is required for the collagen synthesis in the body. Collagen is one of the main structural proteins (inside the body) required for maintaining the integrity of blood vessels, skin, organs, and bones. It would provide sufficient levels of iron, copper, zinc, potassium, manganese, magnesium and selenium. Manganese is used by the body as a cofactor for the antioxidant enzyme, super-oxide dismutase. Selenium is an anti-oxidant trace element required by the human body for smooth heart and liver functions.

In addition cayennepepper.info says: Cayenne Pepper is nothing short of amazing with its effects on the circulatory system as it feeds the vital elements into the cell structure of capillaries, veins, arteries and helps adjust blood pressure to normal levels.

Yes, Capsicum for high blood pressure is certainly one of its core uses, but Capsicum cleans the arteries as well, helping to rid the body of the bad LDL cholesterol and triglycerides. Considering that heart disease is the number one killer in America, this is significant.

Mint

Ahhh beautiful and fragrant mint. The cooling herb.

Digestion:

The health benefits of mint include the following:

- Mint is a great appetizer or palate cleanser, and it promotes digestion.

- It also soothes the stomach in cases of indigestion or inflammation.

- When you feel sick to your stomach, drinking a cup of mint tea can give you relief.

- Also, if you are someone who travels long distances via plane or boat, the menthol oil derived from mint can be very soothing for nausea and related motion sickness.

- The aroma of mint activates the salivary glands in our mouth as well as glands which secrete digestive enzymes, thereby facilitating digestion.

- These attributes are why mint is extensively used in the culinary arts. Much of the Western world includes mint as a part of appetizers or as an element of palate cleansers, to be eaten before the main course so the food will digest comfortably.

- The strong aroma of mint is very effective in clearing up congestion of the nose, throat, bronchi and lungs, which gives relief for respiratory disorders that often result from asthma and the common cold.

- As mint cools and soothes the throat, nose and other respiratory channels, it relieves the irritation which causes chronic coughing.

- And is also used for Asthma.

Organicfacts.net agrees with these findings.

About 460 B.C. "Hippocrates"
known as the father of medicine stated;
"Let thy food be thy medicine"
and these words ring true today.

Now, more than ever when our skies, our soil and our waters
are being polluted, finding a clean source of food is the most
important component we have for our own health and the
health and wellness of our family and loved ones.

Yes, your food is your medicine.
Everyday you make a choice.

This ***"Vibrant Life Cook Book"*** is dedicated to that choice.

Using Foods as Medicine

"We look at some foods as super foods.
The truth is most organically grown vegetables
and spices are "Super Foods"

Super Foods:

We all want to eat the foods that are best for our heart, liver, kidneys and it is always good to know what foods help keep your blood pressure in check and what foods are good for NOT spiking your glucose.

Today, most of the adult population is a bit insulin resistant in varying degrees, which effects the heart, liver and kidneys.
Knowledge is always key.

On the following page is a chart with many foods that are in the *Vibrant Life Cook Book* and some foods that are not. The top foods that have a good impact on your organs and you're "operating systems."
I could not resist sharing this added information with you.

Enjoy

Superfoods Chart

SUPER FOODS	Heart	Liver	Kidney	Blood Sugar	Blood Pressure
Almonds	X				
Apple		X	X		
Apple Cider Vinager				X	
Avocado	X	X	X	X	X
Banana					X
Barley				X	
Beans White					X
Beets		X	X		
Bitter Melon				X	
Bell Peppers					X
Blackberries	X				
Blueberries			X	X	
Broccoli		X	X		X
Cabbage (green and red)		X	X		
Carrots		X	X		
Cauliflower		X			
Cherries				X	
Cinnamon				X	X
Fenugreek					X
Flax Seed	X				
Garlic		X		X	
Grapefruit		X	X		
Green Tea		X			
Kale					X
Kiwifruit					X
Leafy Greens		X	X		
Legumes	X				
Lemons		X	X		
Limes			X		
Nectarines					X
Oatmeal	X				X
Olive Oil	X	X			
Omega 3	X		X		
Onion				X	
Peaches					X
Quinoa					X
Raspberries	X				
Spinach	X		X		
Strawberries	X		X		
Sweet Potato			X		X
Tilapia					X
Turmeric		X			
Walnuts	X		X	X	
Yams				X	

Why these foods are so good for you

Below is some extra added information on 17 top medicinal foods. Why 17?
In numerology the number 17 equals 8.
Eight is the number of prosperity and infinity.

Apples

Apples are high in pectin and hold the chemical constituents necessary for the body to cleanse and release toxins from the digestive tract. This, in turn, makes it easier for the liver to handle the purification system and also helps to cleanse the liver. It is a significant source of antioxidants, including one called quercetin, which is thought to protect brain cells. Fresh apples are also a good source of Vitamin C. Green apples are my choice for a power packed fruit.

Avocados

This nutrient-dense super-food helps the body produce glutathione, a compound that is necessary for the liver to weed out harmful toxins. Avocado is know as the good fat fruit as it also aids the kidneys and may be good for your heart, blood pressure and blood sugar. Avocados are known as a "nutrient booster." They increase the absorption of fat-soluble nutrients like Vitamins A, D, K, and E. They contain 3.5 grams of naturally good fat per 1 oz. serving.

Beets and Carrots

Both are extremely high in plant-flavonoids and beta-carotene; eating beets and carrots can help stimulate and improve overall liver function and kidney function.

Blueberries

Ranked #1 among fresh or frozen fruits and vegetables in antioxidant power, blueberries are a low calorie source of fiber and Vitamin C. They are being studied for their potential to protect against cancer and heart disease and for possible brain health benefits. Eat them raw, mix them in a fruit smoothie or add them to cereal. I like to freeze them and eat like a frozen treat!

Cabbage or Fermented Cabbage

Eating cabbage helps stimulate the activation of two crucial liver detoxifying enzymes that help flush out toxins. ***Try eating more kimchi, coleslaw, cabbage soup and sauerkraut.***

Cruciferous Vegetables

Eating broccoli and cauliflower will increase the amount of glucosinolate in your system, adding to enzyme production in the liver. These natural enzymes help flush out carcinogens, and other toxins out of your body which may significantly lower risks associated with cancer and other degenerative diseases. ***Other liver-loving vegetables include artichoke, asparagus, kale, and brussels sprouts.***

Garlic

Just a small amount of this amazing bulb has the ability to activate liver enzymes that help your body flush out toxins.

Garlic also holds high amounts of allicin and selenium, two natural compounds that aid in liver cleansing and also helps to regulate blood sugar.

Grapefruit

High in both vitamin C and antioxidants, grapefruit increases the natural cleansing processes of the liver. A small glass of freshly squeezed grapefruit juice will help boost production of the liver detoxification enzymes that help flush out carcinogens and other toxins.

Kale

This glorious green is packed with Vitamins A and C, calcium and many other important minerals. Kale is also a serious source of carotenoids and flavonoids, which translates to super eye health and anti-cancer benefits. Kale contains significant sources of Vitamin K. *People taking blood thinners, such as warfarin, should speak to their health care provider before consuming any foods high in Vitamin K. ***Please*** *note* that vitamin K is a coagulant, so if you have had surgery please stay clear for a few months. Kale's peak season is in winter.

Leafy Green Vegetables

One of our most powerful allies in cleansing our bodies, are leafy greens which can be eaten raw, cooked, or juiced. Extremely high in plant chlorophylls, greens suck up environmental toxins from the blood stream. With their distinct ability to neutralize heavy metals, chemicals and pesticides, these cleansing foods offer a powerful protective mechanism for the liver. Incorporating leafy greens such as **bitter gourd, Arugula, dandelion greens, spinach, mustard greens, and chicory** into your diet. Will help increase the creation and flow of bile, the substance that removes waste from the organs and blood.

Lemons and Limes

These citrus fruits contain very high amounts of vitamin C, which aids the body in synthesizing toxic materials into substances that can be absorbed by water. Drinking freshly squeezed lemon or lime juice in the morning helps stimulate the liver.

Olive Oil

Cold-pressed organic oils such as olive, hemp and flax-seed are great for the liver, when used in moderation. They help the body by providing a lipid base that can suck up harmful toxins in the body. In this way, it takes some of the burden off the liver in terms of the toxic overload many of us suffer from.

Spinach

This leafy green vegetable is high in vitamins A, C, K and folate. The beta-carotene found in spinach is important for boosting your immune system health and protecting your vision. It is also a good source of magnesium. Instead of lettuce in your salad, try spinach. You can also easily incorporate spinach into your diet by making a simple side dish of steamed spinach, spiced up with garlic and olive oil. Spinach is considered high potassium food choice.

Sweet Potatoes

Sweet potatoes are packed with beta-carotene and are an excellent source of vitamins A and C. Sweet potatoes are also a good source of vitamin B-6 and potassium. One medium *(5-inch long)* sweet potato contains 112 calories and nearly 4 grams of fiber, according to the *USDA National Nutrient Database*. You can eat them mashed or even make your own oven-baked fries. Sweet potatoes are considered a high potassium food choice.

Turmeric

The liver's favorite spice. Try adding some of this detoxifying goodness into your next lentil stew or veggie dish for an instant liver pick-me-up. Turmeric helps boost liver detox, by assisting enzymes that actively flush out dietary carcinogens. Turmeric is also known for its' anti-inflammatory properties.

Walnuts

Walnuts hold high amounts of the amino acid arginine. Argininee may sometimes trigger the herpes virus (cold sores). Walnuts aid the liver in detoxifying ammonia. Walnuts are also high in glutathione and omega-3 fatty acids, which support normal liver cleansing actions. Make sure you chew the nuts well *(until they are liquified)* before swallowing.

Research includes: AnatomyofHealingandWellness.com, www.kidney.org, www.globalhealingcenter.com, www.livingstrong.com.

Why not Gluten?

We hear so much about *"gluten this"* and *"gluten that,"* it is difficult to decipher through all the hype. And are "gluten free" items always better for you?

I would like to take some time and share with you my take on Gluten and Gluten free.

- Gluten actually means "glue" in Latin.
- Gluten is a combination of proteins found in wheat and wheat related grains like barley, rye oats and others.
- Gluten is used in many products like pastas, cakes, cookies, breads, lunch meats and cereal, just to name a few.

There was a time when our soils were full of minerals and the wheat was growing with clean water and air. The wheat was ground and made into bread and flour. This is NOT the wheat of today! Today the soil is contaminated and absent of minerals. The additives they use to make our products... well, some should be banned. At a record rate people are becoming intolerant to wheat products. This is due to our modern farming practices and the way our products are now made.

The bottom line is, gluten causes inflammation in the body and inflammation has been linked to the increase of all diseases. ***So, when you ingest gluten you increase your risk of diabetes, heart disease and some forms of cancer.*** Gluten turns to sugar in the blood stream, so even if you do not have an allergy it is best to steer clear when you can.

Also, please read labels very carefully. Just because a product says "Gluten Free" does not mean it is free from toxins and chemicals that are not good for your body. So, do your own research on gluten and eat responsibly. We all want to feel great and the body wants to be well. We just have to give our bodies the correct tools.

Here is to your greatest health and most vibrant life!
— Sheila Z

WHEAT FREE DOES NOT ALWAYS MEAN GLUTEN FREE!

Watch for gluten free foods, read labels and be kind to your body.

Below is a list of foods that contain Gluten:

- Rye
- Barley
- Wheat
- Spelt
- Bread
- Bread Crumbs
- Pasta
- Fried Foods
- Cous Cous
- Matza
- Cereal
- Self-basting Turkey
- Processed Meats
- Pasta Mixes
- Soy Sauce
- Oats *(pure oats are gluten free)*
- Chocolates containing malt
- Many Salad Dressings
- Whiskey and Beer
- Any Snacks or Sweets that have flour in it
- Candies *(containing cereal extract, root beers)*
- Many other Processed Foods

About the Author

Sheila is more than an award winning author, amazing whole food chef and creator of these wonderful recipes. Sheila is dedicated to helping people live healthier lives. Her connection to mother nature and her respect for the land and all living things is unique and filled with wisdom beyond her years. Sheila has helped countless people worldwide gain a deeper understanding to the causes of their life challenges.

Sheila is . . .

- A PhD in Natural Health/Philosophy
- An Emotional Clarity Specialist
- Certified Lymphologist
- Master Meditation Instructor
- Certified Light & Sound Healer
- Creator of *True Life Solutions* & *"The Intentional Wellness Experience™"*
- An International Inspirational Speaker & Catalyst for Youngevity

- Reiki Master
- Energy Specialist
- Ordained Minister
- Intuitive
- Acutonics Practitioner
- Developed the Vibrant Life Protocol™
- Certified Nutritional Live Blood Microscopist

Join us for a 3 day transformational retreat or an all day experience.
From Ancient Ways to Quantum Physics. All the pieces of the puzzle.

Through years of study and working with clients, Sheila has become an expert in emotional clarity and is a catalyst for healing and wellness. She is a Spiritual Evolutionist, and has an on-going practice in Las Vegas, Nevada. Sheila is a Healing, Wellness, and Relationship coach. Her meditations have helped countless people find their gifts and their purpose. She has enriched the lives of many with her insights and grace.

Anatomy of Healing and Wellness

268 full color pages of ways to improve your Health and Wellness. An in depth guide, resource and cutting edge information on how to stay 30 till you are 90! From Physical form of Wellness to the Science of Wellness and the Emotional aspect of Wellness. Using foods as medicine and so much more.

"This book is amazing as it shows you what herbs, teas and natural sources can help to heal whatever ails you. A great book on preventing illness and on recovery."

$29.95   To order, please go to: www.Truelife-solutions.com

Stirling's Vibrant Life Protocol

Can you change your health in 100 days? YES! Vastly improve the conditions of your blood and get your body back into balance. This program is not for the faint of heart. If you want to avoid illness, want to strengthen your system and stay "30 til you are 90" this is the program for you.   An in-depth discovery session is required before starting this protocol. Each protocol is explicitly for one person. You! Contact Dr. Stirling for an apt.

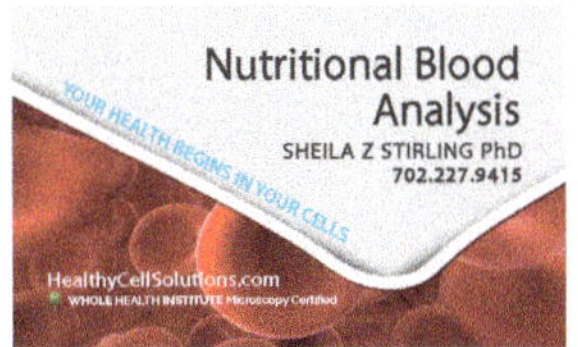

Dr. Stirling is certified in "Nutritional Live Blood Microscopy"
You can email her for an appointment: info@HealthyCellSolutions.com

Recovering from Hip Pinning Surgery

This amazing full color booklet gives you important
information and a step-by-step guide on how to best recover from major surgery like hip pinning. A useful guide and inspiration for those going into a surgical procedure.
$4.95 To order please go to www.Truelife-solutions.com.

Sounds of the Soul CD

When listened through headphones, this CD seems to balance Alpha, Beta, Theta, and Delta brainwaves. The implications of this are boundless and as we know that meditation has the ability to decrease blood pressure and stress levels. We now know that *Sounds of the Soul* may potentially normalize brain function and, in doing so, heal the body on a cellular and soulular level. The sounds and tones are very relaxing and channel directly to the soul, so open your heart and breathe in the music. Many have experienced a reconnection with spirit and accelerated healing.

Cutting edge scientific studies are now being done with neuro-feedback EEGs and the initial findings are astounding. *Sounds of the Soul* was channeled from the celestial realm through Sheila Z. It is an interpretation of the God code of creation in collaboration with Gary Stadler of HeartMagic Studios. There are 2 tracks on this CD one is 18:50 minutes and the other is 27:24 minutes.

To order, please go to: www.Truelife-solutions.com - click on "Store" and listen to a Free clip of the CD. $15 plus $5 shipping within the United States

Deep Healing Meditation with The Sounds of the Soul CD

This is a journey meditation that encourages your connection to the healer within. Building the healing energy of the cosmos and being in the heightened vibrations of the angelic realms from *Sounds of the Soul*. This meditation is about 27 minutes.

To order please go to www.Truelife-solutions.com.
$19.95 plus $4 shipping within the United States.

True Life Solutions

Sheila Z Stirling is dedicated to healing the planet and raising the consciousness of humanity. This has been a diverse journey, from Ancient ways to Quantum Physics, from Philosophy to Alchemy. Below are web sites created by Sheila Z Stirling for the advancement, education and accelerated healing for all. Sheila is an Environmental Activist and has lobbied for the national parks in Washington D.C. Sheila is the Southern Nevada coordinator for the *Institute of Noetic Sciences - Bridging Science and Consciousness.*

Sheila Z's sites:

TrueLife-Solutions.com - Sheila Z's main web site on health and wellness.

TrueEMFSolutions.com - This site is dedicated to protection from EMF's.

TheEwellnessstore.com - This site has the tried and true health products that are the favorites of True Life-Solutions and Sheila Z.

YosemiteEbook.com - A beautiful book about Yosemite, photos and writings by Sheila Z.

LoveandIllusion.com - This award winning book written by Dr. Stirling covers the subject of sociopathic behavior in relationships.

IONSLasVegas.com - The site for the community group "Bridging Science and Consciousness."

ZenGems.net - Healing Stone Jewelry designed and created by Sheila Z.

Whatsupwithplanetearth.org - Information on Mother Earth.

AnatomyofHealingandWellness.com - The website for Sheila Z's amazing holistic health resource book.

" Sheila Z Stirling is a wonderful presenter, inspirational motivational speaker.
Her knowledge of the human form and the path to regain complete wellness has
helped achieve great success for so many. Please contact Sheila for more information on having
her speak at your group, company gathering. Consider booking an in-depth Discovery session. I
understand it can be life changing for the better. I have known
Dr. Stirling for many years and have experienced and benefited from her knowledge,
her wisdom and her teachings."
— Dr. Stephen Ezra West, DL - www.zerodisease.com